T0285147

Crowds in American Culture, Society, and Politics

Crowds in American Culture, Society, and Politics

A Psychosocial Semiotic Analysis

Arthur Asa Berger

ANTHEM PRESS

Anthem Press
An imprint of Wimbledon Publishing Company
www.anthempress.com

This edition first published in UK and USA 2023
by ANTHEM PRESS
75–76 Blackfriars Road, London SE1 8HA, UK
or PO Box 9779, London SW19 7ZG, UK
and
244 Madison Ave #116, New York, NY 10016, USA

British Library Cataloguing-in-Publication Data
A catalogue record for this book is available from the British Library.

Library of Congress Cataloging-in-Publication Data
A catalog record for this book has been requested.
2022951923

ISBN-13: 978-1-83998-860-8 (Pbk)
ISBN-10: 1-83998-860-6 (Pbk)

This title is also available as an e-book.

CONTENTS

Since its first publication in the French language in 1895, *The Crowd: A Study of the Popular Mind* (French: Psychologie des Foules; literally: Psychology of Crowds) has offered a penetrating, profound study of an important being or phenomenon of the present age, the crowd, and thus been one of the most influential small books in the world today. Even when we read it today, more than a century after its first publication, Le Bon's book addresses readers and problems of our epoch as it did to readers and problems a century ago. In our age of democracy, the activities of crowds are playing more and more important roles, particularly when we extend the concept of the crowd to cover not only political crowds, but also religious, ethnic, racial, or even gender crowds. In our time, "organized crowds have always played an important part in the life of peoples" as it did a century ago (p.5). In our time, "the destinies of nations of nations are elaborated at present in the heart of the masses, and no longer in the councils of princes." (p.15). Meanwhile, in our time, "the substitution of the unconscious action of crowds for the conscious activity of the individual is one of the principal characteristics of the present age", as it was a century ago (p.5). Of course, the crowd phenomenon is not only characteristic of totalitarian regimes. It is also characteristic of any democratic society, including those most matured ones in North America and Europe.

Review by Barabara Entl, MD. *Journal of East-West Thought.*
Accessed 12/4/2021.

Users/arthu/Downloads/2369-Article%20Text-3839-1-10-20200413%20(2).pdf

Chapter 1

INTRODUCTION

This book is about the role of crowds in American society, culture, and politics. It offers a detailed description of Gustave Le Bon's *The Crowd: A Study of the Popular Mind* (published in English in 1896 and thus in the public domain), and a discussion of Sigmund Freud's 1921 book on group psychology, among other things.

I use so much from Le Bon that it might be correct to cite him as a coauthor of this book, but I quote him because his ideas are central to my argument and I want my readers to be able to see, in some depth, what he had to say about crowds.

I also make extended use of material from Wikipedia on a variety of topics. I like Wikipedia because it offers valuable overviews and readable discussions on many topics of interest to me in this book. I recognize that some academics frown on using material from Wikipedia, but I have always found its articles extremely useful.

This book deals with some important aspects of American society, politics, and culture. It seeks to answer questions such as what do Trump's followers (his crowds) see in him and why did so many people become insurrectionists on January 6, 2021, and try to prevent the counting of the electoral votes leading to the election of Joe Biden, and attack the Capitol? I also consider crowds and cults and the role of crowds in COVID and vaccine hesitancy and opposition to vaccinations in the United States and elsewhere (Figure 1.1).

In my books, I like to use quotations from authors so that my readers can see how authors expressed themselves. Except for the material from Le Bon's book, and Wikipedia, the quotations in this book are all less than 350 words and thus qualify as fair use, and I give credit to the writers for all materials that I quote. My book has, then, something of a documentary quality about it. We can think of the quotations I use as the equivalent of statements by expert witnesses in a trial.

The classic text on crowds is Gustave Le Bon's *The Crowd*, first published in 1895 in French and 1896 in English. It is recognized as one of the most

Figure 1.1 January 6, 2021 Riot at the Capitol. Photo by the Author from Television.

Figure 1.2 Gustave Le Bon. Drawing by the Author.

important social psychology studies ever published and my book is an application of Le Bon's ideas about crowds to contemporary American society, politics, and culture.

The noun "crowd" is defined in the *Merriam-Webster's Collegiate Dictionary* 10th Edition as follows:

> 1: a large number of persons esp. when collected together: THRONG. 2: a: the great body of people: POPULACE b. close together. 3: most of one's peers…3: a large number of things close together 4: a group of people having something (as a habit, interest, or occupation) in common…..*syn* CROWD, THRONG, CRUSH, MOB, HORDE mean an assembled multitude usu. of people. CROWD implies a close gathering and pressing together….MOB implies a disorderly crowd with the potential for violence….

We can see from the length of this definition that the term "crowd" is a complicated one to understand. One question involving crowds is—how many people do you need to make a group? And how many people are needed for a group of people to become a crowd? Also, is there a significant difference between small crowds and large ones? In the next chapter, I will discuss, in some detail, the most important ideas in the book and quote key passages in some depth. Subsequent chapters will deal with various aspects of crowds and crowds in America, or what I call American "variants" of crowds.

Charles-Marie Gustave Le Bon (French: [gystav lə bɔ̃]; 7 May 1841—13 December 1931) was a leading French polymath whose areas of interest included anthropology, psychology, sociology, medicine, invention, and physics.[1][2][3] He is best known for his 1895 work *The Crowd: A Study of the Popular Mind*, which is considered one of the seminal works of crowd psychology.

In the 1890s, he turned to psychology and sociology, in which fields he released his most successful works. Le Bon developed the view that crowds are not the sum of their individual parts, proposing that within crowds there forms a new psychological entity, the characteristics of which are determined by the "racial unconscious" of the crowd. At the same time, he created his psychological and sociological theories, he performed experiments in physics, and published popular books on the subject, anticipating the mass–energy equivalence and prophesizing the Atomic Age. Le Bon maintained his eclectic interests up until his death in 1931.

Ignored or maligned by sections of the French academic and scientific establishment during his life due to his politically conservative and reactionary views, Le Bon was critical of democracy and socialism. Le Bon's works were influential to such disparate figures as Theodore Roosevelt, Benito Mussolini, Sigmund Freud, José Ortega y Gasset, Adolf Hitler, and Vladimir Lenin.

https://en.wikipedia.org

Chapter 2

THE CROWD

Le Bon's book, *The Crowd: A Study of the Popular Mind*, was published in English in 1896 by Macmillan. I will use quotes from that edition in this book. In 1960, an edition of *The Crowd* was published by the Viking Press with a long introduction by Robert K. Merton, an important sociologist. I will discuss Merton's ideas at the end of this chapter.

Organization of *The Crowd*

Introduction:
The Era of Crowds

Book I
The Mind of Crowds

Chapter 1
General Characteristics of Crowds
Chapter 2
The Sentiments and Morality of Crowds
Chapter 3
The Ideas, Reasoning Power, and Imagination of Crowds
Chapter 4
A Religious Shape Assume by All the Convictions of Crowds

Book II
The Opinions and Beliefs of Crowds

Chapter 1
Remote Factors of the Opinions and Beliefs of Crowds
Chapter 2
The Immediate Factors of the Opinions of Crowds

We can see from this table of contents that Le Bon cast a wide net and there aren't many aspects of crowds that he did not consider. For my purposes, some material in his chapters is very important for us to consider and I offer this material in extended excerpts.

I will now discuss some of Le Bon's key ideas and quote some of the most important passages from the 1896 edition of his book.

Le Bon's Definition of Crowds

1.
Le Bon begins chapter 1 of Book I with his definition of crowds (1896: 1,2):

IN its ordinary sense the word "crowd" means a gathering of individuals of whatever nationality, profession, or sex, and whatever be the chances that have brought them together. From the psychological point of view, the expression "crowd" assumes quite a different signification. Under certain given circumstances, and only under those circumstances, an agglomeration of men presents new characteristics very different from those of the individuals composing it. The sentiments and ideas of all the persons in the gathering take one and the same direction, and their conscious personality vanishes. A collective mind is formed, doubtless transitory, but presenting very clearly defined characteristics. The gathering has thus become what, in the absence of a better expression, I will call an organised crowd, or, if the term is considered preferable, a psychological crowd. It forms a single being, and is subjected to the law of the mental unity of crowds.

Le Bon points out that under certain circumstances, the "sentiments and ideas" of all the individuals in the crowd become similar and form a collective mind and the gathering becomes an organized or psychological crowd, much different from the individuals who form the crowd.

People in a crowd lose their individuality and the crowd affects their thought processes.

Hidden Motives in Crowds

2.
This loss of individuality happens because (1896: 9):

> The greater part of our daily actions are the result of hidden motives which escape our observation.

It is these unconscious factors that enable people, who in many respects differ greatly from one another, to form a group mind and lose their individuality. This phenomenon suggests a psychoanalytic perspective and, as we shall see, Sigmund Freud read Le Bon's book and commented on his ideas. As Le Bon explains (1896: 13):

> We see, then, that the disappearance of the conscious personality, the predominance of the unconscious personality, the turning by means of suggestion and contagion of feelings and ideas in an identical direction, the tendency to immediately transform the suggested ideas into acts; these, we see, are the principal characteristics of the individual forming part of a crowd. He is no longer himself, but has become an automaton who has ceased to be guided by his will. Moreover, by the mere fact that he forms part of an organised crowd, a man descends several rungs in the ladder of civilisation. Isolated, he may be a cultivated individual; in a crowd, he is a barbarian

In crowds, Le Bon explains, we lose our individuality and independence and gain a sense of power from the crowd that enables us to do things, as members of a crowd, we would never do as individuals.

Figure 2.1 The crowd at the January 6 riot.

The Role of Images and Contagion in Crowds

3.

Le Bon discusses the role of images and their role in fostering contagion in crowds (1896: 23–24):

> A crowd thinks in images, and the image itself immediately calls up a series of other images, having no logical connection with the first. We can easily conceive this state by thinking of the fantastic succession of ideas to which we are sometimes led by calling up in our minds any fact. Our reason shows us the incoherence there is in these images, but a crowd is almost blind to this truth, and confuses with the real event what the deforming action of its imagination has superimposed thereon. A crowd scarcely distinguishes between the subjective and the objective. It accepts as real the images evoked in its mind, though they most often have only a very distant relation with the observed fact. The ways in which a crowd perverts any event of which it is a witness ought, it would seem, to be innumerable and unlike each other, since the individuals composing the gathering are of very different temperaments. But this is not the case. As the result of contagion, the perversions are of the same kind, and take the same shape in the case of all the assembled individuals.

Crowds, Le Bon argues, are blind to the truth and cannot differentiate between the real and the imagined. While the members of the crowd are all individuals, as a result of the contagion, they share beliefs with other members of the crowd. This notion is similar to what communications scholars described as the "magic bullet" theory, which argued that all viewers of mass-mediated texts get the same message. It is now discredited.

The Magic Bullet or Hypodermic Needle Theory of Communication

Wikipedia explains the "magic bullet" theory:

> The "Magic Bullet" or "Hypodermic Needle Theory" of direct influence effects was based on early observations of the effect of mass media, as used by Nazi propaganda and the effects of Hollywood in the 1930s and 1940s.[1] People were assumed to be "uniformly controlled by their biologically based 'instincts' and that they react more or less uniformly to whatever 'stimuli' came along".[2] The "Magic Bullet" theory graphically assumes that the media's message is a bullet fired from the "media gun" into the viewer's "head".[3] Similarly, the "Hypodermic Needle Model" uses the same idea of the "shooting" paradigm. It suggests that the media injects its messages straight into the passive audience.[4] This passive audience is immediately affected by these messages. The public essentially cannot escape from the media's influence, and is therefore considered a "sitting duck".[4] Both models suggest that the public is vulnerable to the messages shot at them because of the limited communication tools and the studies of the media's effects on the masses at the time.[5] It means the media explores information in such a way that it injects in the mind of audiences as bullets.
>
> (https://en.wikipedia.org/wiki/Magic_bullet_theory)

We will see that Le Bon has ideas quite similar to this theory to explain the behavior of crowds.

The Exaggeration of Feelings through Violent Affirmations in Crowds

4.
Here, Le Bon deals with the exaggeration of feelings found in crowds, the way orators abusively use violent affirmations, repeat themselves constantly, and don't make use of reasoning in moving crowds (1896: 36–37):

> Given to exaggeration in its feelings, a crowd is only impressed by excessive sentiments. An orator wishing to move a crowd must make an abusive use of violent affirmations. To exaggerate, to affirm,

to resort to repetitions, and never to attempt to prove anything by reasoning are methods of argument well known to speakers at public meetings. Moreover, a crowd exacts a like exaggeration in the sentiments of its heroes. Their apparent qualities and virtues must always be amplified. It has been justly remarked that on the stage a crowd demands from the hero of the piece a degree of courage, morality, and virtue that is never to be found in real life. Quite rightly importance has been laid on the special standpoint from which matters are viewed in the theatre. Such a standpoint exists no doubt, but its rules for the most part have nothing to do with common sense and logic. The art of appealing to crowds is no doubt of an inferior order, but it demands quite special aptitudes. It is often impossible on reading plays to explain their success. Managers of theatres when accepting pieces are themselves, as a rule, very uncertain of their success, because to judge the matter it would be necessary that they should be able to transform themselves into a crowd.

The Lack of Morality in Crowds

5.

Here Le Bon discusses the matter of the morality or, more precisely, the lack of morality of crowds. The individuals who make up crowds may have a sense of morality when they are on their own, but when they are in crowds, they abandon their sense of morality. As Le Bon explains (1896: 43):

Taking the word "morality" to mean constant respect for certain social conventions, and the permanent repression of selfish impulses, it is quite evident that crowds are too impulsive and too mobile to be moral. If, however, we include in the term morality the transitory display of certain qualities such as abnegation, self-sacrifice, disinterestedness, devotion, and the need of equity, we may say, on the contrary, that crowds may exhibit at times a very lofty morality. The few psychologists who have studied crowds have only considered them from the point of view of their criminal acts, and noticing how frequent these acts are, they have come to the conclusion that the moral standard of crowds is very low. Doubtless this is often the case; but why? Simply because our savage, destructive instincts are the inheritance left dormant in all of us from the primitive ages. In the life of the isolated individual it would be dangerous for him to gratify these instincts, while his absorption in an irresponsible crowd, in which in consequence he is assured of impunity, gives him entire liberty to follow them.

Figure 2.2 Trump rally. Photo by the author taken from television.

Le Bon adds that crowds are also capable of incredible acts of heroism, the other side of the morality coin, but it is their negative behavior that is of most interest to us. He ascribes the capacity for violence and our destructive instincts to residues in people's psyches from the primitive ages. It is part of what we might call the collective unconscious that unites people in their capacity for immoral, violent, and antisocial behavior.

The Power of Images on Crowds

6.

Here we return to Le Bon's ideas about the power of images (1896: 57):

> Appearances have always played a much more important part than reality in history, where the unreal is always of greater moment than the real. Crowds being only capable of thinking in images are only to be impressed by images. It is only images that terrify or attract them and become motives of action. For this reason theatrical representations, in which the image is shown in its most clearly visible shape, always have an enormous influence on crowds. Bread and spectacular shows constituted for the plebeians of ancient Rome the ideal of happiness, and they asked for nothing more. Throughout the successive ages this ideal has scarcely varied. Nothing has a greater effect on the imagination of crowds of every category than theatrical representations. The entire audience experiences at the same time the same emotions, and if these

Figure 2.3 The American flag.

emotions are not at once transformed into acts, it is because the most unconscious spectator cannot ignore that he is the victim of illusions, and that he has laughed or wept over imaginary adventures.

Le Bon's suggestion that everyone in an audience experiences the same emotions at the same time is similar to the "magic bullet" or "hypodermic needle" theory of communication, discussed earlier in this chapter. But while his notion may be a bit extreme, it is also often the case that most people in the audiences of theatrical presentations, and crowds of one sort or another, do feel very similar feelings and emotions.

Images have enormous power and people sometimes sacrifice their lives to fight for the values and beliefs reflected in images. Think, for example, of the people who join the United States Army or Marines or other branches of the military services to support the American flag and all that it represents in their minds.

The Religious Sentiment Found in Crowds

7.

Le Bon deals with what he calls the "religious sentiment" and describes what we might call the basic elements found in cults in contemporary societies (1896: 63):

> This sentiment has very simple characteristics, such as worship of a being supposed superior, fear of the power with which the being is credited,

blind submission to its commands, inability to discuss its dogmas, the desire to spread them, and a tendency to consider as enemies all by whom they are not accepted. Whether such a sentiment apply to an invisible God, to a wooden or stone idol, to a hero or to a political conception, provided that it presents the preceding characteristics, its essence always remains religious. The supernatural and the miraculous are found to be present to the same extent. Crowds unconsciously accord a mysterious power to the political formula or the victorious leader that for the moment arouses their enthusiasm. A person is not religious solely when he worships a divinity, but when he puts all the resources of his mind, the complete submission of his will, and the whole-souled ardour of fanaticism at the service of a cause or an individual who becomes the goal and guide of his thoughts and actions. Intolerance and fanaticism are the necessary accompaniments of the religious sentiment. They are inevitably displayed by those who believe themselves in the possession of the secret of earthly or eternal happiness. These two characteristics are to be found in all men grouped together when they are inspired by a conviction of any kind. The Jacobins of the Reign of Terror were at bottom as religious as the Catholics of the Inquisition, and their cruel ardour proceeded from the same source. The convictions of crowds assume those characteristics of blind submission, fierce intolerance, and the need of violent propaganda which are inherent in the religious sentiment, and it is for this reason that it may be said that all their beliefs have a religious form. The hero acclaimed by a crowd is a veritable god for that crowd.

We can understand, now, why crowds feel the way they do about their leaders and see them as God-like figures. A contemporary American cult, QAnon, sees Trump as sent by the Gods to lead the fight against Democratic politicians who are seen as pedophiles. Recall that in one rally, Trump said, "I alone can save you."

Wikipedia describes QAnon as follows:

QAnon[a] (/ˌkjuːəˈnɒn/) is a far-right conspiracy movement centered on false claims made by an anonymous individual or individuals, known by the name "Q", that a cabal of Satanic,[1] cannibalistic pedophiles operate a global child sex trafficking ring and conspired against former President Donald Trump during his term in office. QAnon has been described as a cult. One shared belief among QAnon members is that Trump was planning a massive sting operation on the cabal, with mass arrests of thousands of cabal members to take place on a day known as the "Storm," QAnon supporters have accused many Hollywood actors, Democratic politicians, and high-ranking government officials of being members of the cabal, without providing evidence.

(https://en.wikipedia.org/wiki/QAnon)

Evidence and proofs are of no concern to the heroes of groups and a particular and pernicious form of groups—cults. When a crowd becomes a cult is difficult to say, but there is reason to suggest that many followers of Trump, including members of the U.S. House of Representatives and the U.S. Senate, are, in fact, members of a cult led by Trump. Within that cult, you have another subcult, QAnon, for the most extreme true believers.

Discontent and Grievances in Crowds

8.

Le Bon argues that the overproduction of educated people leads to serious problems. As he explains, discussing the system of education in most countries, the educational system generates unhappiness in most people that has negative consequences (1896: 86–88):

> But the system presents a far more serious danger. It gives those who have been submitted to it a violent dislike to the state of life in which they were born, and an intense desire to escape from it. The working man no longer wishes to remain a working man, or the peasant to continue a peasant, while the most humble members of the middle classes admit of no possible career for their sons except that of State-paid functionaries. Instead of preparing men for life French schools solely prepare them to occupy public functions, in which success can be attained without any necessity for self-direction or the exhibition of the least glimmer of personal initiative. At the bottom of the social ladder the system creates an army of proletarians discontented with their lot and always ready to revolt, while at the summit it brings into being a frivolous bourgeoisie, at once sceptical and credulous, having a superstitious confidence in the State, whom it regards as a sort of Providence, but without forgetting to display towards it a ceaseless hostility, always laying its own faults to the door of the Government, and incapable of the least enterprise without the intervention of the authorities.

Many academics, writers, and politicians commented on the unrealistic reliance we had on the institutions of the government to protect us from the assault on widely accepted governmental norms that took place during the Trump presidency. The followers of Trump identified with his attacks on the press and his continual attempts to undermine the institutions of government which were, in many cases, successful. What Le Bon does in this passage is help explain the feelings of grievances that animated Trump and his followers.

Images, Words, and Formulas Used by Orators

9.

Le Bon returns to his interest in images in a discussion of images, words, and formulas in his chapter on immediate factors of the opinions of crowds. He deals with the power of language and the techniques orators use, such as exaggeration and repetition, to excite crowds (1896: 100–103):

> The power of words is bound up with the images they evoke, and is quite independent of their real significance. Words whose sense is the most ill-defined are sometimes those that possess the most influence. Such, for example, are the terms democracy, socialism, equality, liberty, &c., whose meaning is so vague that bulky volumes do not suffice to precisely fix it….The images evoked by words being independent of their sense, they vary from age to age and from people to people, the formulas remaining identical. Certain transitory images are attached to certain words: the word is merely as it were the button of an electric bell that calls them up. All words and all formulas do not possess the power of evoking images, while there are some which have once had this power, but lose it in the course of use, and cease to waken any response in the mind. They then become vain sounds, whose principal utility is to relieve the person who employs them of the obligation of thinking. Armed with a small stock of formulas and commonplaces learnt while we are young, we possess all that is needed to traverse life without the tiring necessity of having to reflect on anything whatever.

Le Bon calls our attention to the power of certain words to generate certain images and emotions in the minds of people that generate beliefs in crowds. These words often are vague and hard to define, but they shape the thinking of people in crowds. This exaggeration and repetition is found in Trump's rhetoric, which is similar in many respects to the rhetoric used by the Nazis in Germany.

Political scientists have found that people often repeat "talking points" of political parties when they discuss issues, often having unconsciously memorized catchphrases used by political parties in their advertisements and radio and television commercials.

In contemporary American politics, in 2022, we have some crowds of people yelling "Stop the Steal" and other crowds complaining about "The Big Lie." Le Bon asserts that orators addressing crowds always appeal to their feelings, emotions, and sentiments and never to their reason.

The Importance of Repetition

10.
Le Bon asserts that affirmation, kept free of reasoning, and repetition, which generate contagion, are crucial techniques used by orators when addressing crowds. In his discussion of "The Leaders of Crowds," he writes (1896: 126–127):

> Affirmation, however, has no real influence unless it be constantly repeated, and so far as possible in the same terms. It was Napoleon, I believe, who said that there is only one figure in rhetoric of serious importance, namely, repetition. The thing affirmed comes by repetition to fix itself in the mind in such a way that it is accepted in the end as a demonstrated truth. The influence of repetition on crowds is comprehensible when the power is seen which it exercises on the most enlightened minds.
>
> This power is due to the fact that the repeated statement is embedded in the long run in those profound regions of our unconscious selves in which the motives of our actions are forged. At the end of a certain time we have forgotten who is the author of the repeated assertion, and we finish by believing it. To this circumstance is due the astonishing power of advertisements.
>
> When we have read a hundred, a thousand, times that X's chocolate is the best, we imagine we have heard it said in many quarters, and we end by acquiring the certitude that such is the fact. When we have read a thousand times that Y's pills have cured the most illustrious persons of the most obstinate maladies, we are tempted at last to try them when suffering from an illness of a similar kind. If we always read in the same papers that A is an arrant scamp and B a most honest man, we end up being convinced that this is the truth, unless, indeed, we are given to reading another paper of the contrary opinion, in which the two qualifications are reversed. Affirmation and repetition are alone powerful enough to combat each other.

Le Bon argued that when people are gathered together in crowds, emotions become contagious and reason flies out the door, so to speak. Affirmation, repetition, and contagion, he asserted, become dominant in crowds, a process he called obtaining prestige.

Le Bon recognized the power of advertising when he wrote the book. Since 1895, when the book was published, advertising has become increasingly important in politics and politicians devote a great deal of time and effort to getting funds to finance their advertising campaigns. In the 2020 presidential election, a group of Republicans who disliked Trump got together, formed an advertising agency, *The Lincoln Project*, and promoted many anti-Trump television commercials.

One of their most brilliant commercials, "Covita," based on the musical play "Evita," had numerous images attacking Trump, such as the one below that dealt with his continual lying. *The Washington Post* estimates that Trump told 30,000 misstatements and lies while in office.

This image is from the anti-Trump "Covita" commercial, which involves tying together the Covid plague and Evita, the Broadway show. The commercial is based on a revision of the song "Don't Cry for Me, Argentina." The Lincoln Project is still making anti-Republican commercials, which means anti-Trump (since he still controls the Republican Party) commercials. It sees the Republican Party and Trump as threats to American democracy.

Figure 2.4 Image from anti-Trump "Covita" commercial.

The Importance of Prestige

11.

In his discussion of electoral crowds, Le Bon explains why prestige is so important for political candidates. He writes (1896: 190–191):

> It is of primary importance that the candidate should possess prestige. Personal prestige can only be replaced by that resulting from wealth. Talent and even genius are not elements of success of serious importance. Of capital importance, on the other hand, is the necessity for the candidate of possessing prestige, of being able, that is, to force himself upon the electorate without discussion. The reason why the electors, of whom a majority are working men or peasants, so rarely choose a man from their own ranks to represent them is that such a person enjoys no prestige among them. When, by chance, they do elect a man who is their equal, it is as a rule for subsidiary reasons – for instance, to spite an eminent man, or an influential employer of labour on whom the elector is in daily dependence, and whose master he has the illusion he becomes in this way for a moment.
>
> The possession of prestige does not suffice, however, to assure the success of a candidate. The elector stickles in particular for the flattery of his greed and vanity. He must be overwhelmed with the most extravagant blandishments, and there must be no hesitation in making him the most fantastic promises. If he is a working man it is impossible to go too far in insulting and stigmatising employers of labour. As for the rival candidate, an effort must be made to destroy his chance by establishing by dint of affirmation, repetition, and contagion that he is an arrant scoundrel, and that it is a matter of common knowledge that he has been guilty of several crimes. It is, of course, useless to trouble about any semblance of proof. Should the adversary be ill-acquainted with the psychology of crowds he will try to justify himself by arguments instead of confining himself to replying to one set of affirmations by another; and he will have no chance whatever of being successful.
>
> The candidate's written programme should not be too categorical, since later on his adversaries might bring it up against him; in his verbal programme, however, there cannot be too much exaggeration. The most important reforms may be fearlessly promised. At the moment they are made these exaggerations produce a great effect, and they are not binding for the future, it being a matter of constant observation that the elector never troubles himself to know how far the candidate

he has returned has followed out the electoral programme he applauded, and in virtue of which the election was supposed to have been secured.

Le Bon's description of the way political leaders make "the most fantastic promises" that are not binding shows how profound his understanding of human psychology was. These promises have a powerful impact on members of a crowd, but the exited crowd does not hold the politician to his promises, as a rule.

Aristotle offered some ideas about persuasion that are worth considering. In his *Rhetoric* Book 1, chapter 2 (in McKeon, 1951: 1329), he writes:

Of the modes of persuasion furnished by the spoken word there are three kinds. The first depends upon the personal character of the speaker; the second on putting the audience into a certain frame of mind; the third on the proof or apparent proof, provided by the words of the speech itself.

Figure 2.5 Aristotle.

Aristotle on Persuasion

There are, Aristotle argues, three modes of persuasion based on:

Ethos
The personal character, that is the prestige, of the speaker.

Pathos
The way the speaker stirs emotions in listeners.

Logos
The logical arguments made by the speaker.

Le Bon does not consider the logical arguments made by speakers to be of much importance and focuses on the ethos, the prestige of the speakers, and on the pathos, the way the speakers stir emotions in audiences.

On Leaders

12.

In his last chapter, on parliamentary assemblies, Le Bon suggests that parliaments are the best form of government. He deals with the personality of leaders and has some interesting ideas about leadership and intelligence. Leaders who are too intelligent generally cannot connect with the public. As Le Bon explains (1896: 213–214):

> On occasion, the leader may be intelligent and highly educated, but the possession of these qualities does him, as a rule, more harm than good. By showing how complex things are, by allowing of explanation and promoting comprehension, intelligence always renders its owner indulgent, and blunts, in a large measure, that intensity and violence of conviction needful for apostles. The great leaders of crowds of all ages, and those of the Revolution in particular, have been of lamentably narrow intellect; while it is precisely those whose intelligence has been the most restricted who have exercised the greatest influence.
>
> The speeches of the most celebrated of them, of Robespierre, frequently astound one by their incoherence: by merely reading them no plausible explanation is to be found of the great part played by the powerful dictator.... It is terrible at times to think of the power that strong conviction combined with extreme narrowness of mind gives a man possessing prestige. It is none the less necessary that these

Figure 2.6 Trump rally. Photo by the author taken from television.

conditions should be satisfied for a man to ignore obstacles and display strength of will in a high measure.

It is remarkable how Le Bon's description of leaders still makes sense and describes the personality (a lamentably narrow intellect) and oratory (incoherent and generally inflammatory) of Donald Trump (who is not supposed to be very intelligent and may even be stupid) and many other politicians.

The Decline of Race

13.
Le Bon writes, in the final chapter in his book, on parliamentary assemblies, and how the intermingling of races and the necessities of life form a race, an aggregate that he suggests has common characteristics and sentiments. The crowd becomes, eventually, a people who can escape from their barbarous state and form a new civilization. But there are always forces attacking this new entity—such as individualism. As he explains in the last paragraphs in his book (1896: 229–230):

> With the progressive perishing of its ideal the race loses more and more the qualities that lent it its cohesion, its unity, and its strength. The personality and intelligence of the individual may increase, but at the same time this collective egoism of the race is replaced by an excessive development of the egoism of the individual, accompanied

by a weakening of character and a lessening of the capacity for action. What constituted a people, a unity, a whole, becomes in the end an agglomeration of individualities lacking cohesion, and artificially held together for a time by its traditions and institutions. It is at this stage that men, divided by their interests and aspirations, and incapable any longer of self-government, require directing in their pettiest acts, and that the State exerts an absorbing influence.

With the definite loss of its old ideal the genius of the race entirely disappears; it is a mere swarm of isolated individuals and returns to its original state – that of a crowd. Without consistency and without a future, it has all the transitory characteristics of crowds. Its civilisation is now without stability, and at the mercy of every chance. The populace is sovereign, and the tide of barbarism mounts. The civilisation may still seem brilliant because it possesses an outward front, the work of a long past, but it is in reality an edifice crumbling to ruin, which nothing supports, and destined to fall in at the first storm. To pass in pursuit of an ideal from the barbarous to the civilised state, and then, when this ideal has lost its virtue, to decline and die, such is the cycle of the life of a people.

Le Bon's description of a state withering and ending up as a "mere swarm of isolated individuals" seems to describe much of American politics today. Le Bon believed states were victims of life cycles and that states eventually self-destruct because of the acid of particularism and individualism. In a sense, Le Bon describes what conservative politicians call "replacement theory," which is that people of color will replace white people in America and it will resemble a typical third world country. Racism continues to be a major problem in America, where white supremacist movements have been growing increasingly strong.

The questions we must ask, here, are: was Le Bon right, and was he predicting what would happen in America?

Le Bon made an argument similar to that of De Tocqueville, who argues in his book, *Democracy in America*, published in 1835, that egalitarian states always must deal with the problem of individualism. As he explains (1956: 192–193):

Individualism is a mature and calm feeling, which disposes each member of the community to sever himself from the mass of his fellows, and to draw apart with his family and friends; so that, after he has thus formed a little circle of his own, he willingly leaves society at large to itself. Selfishness originates in blind instinct; individualism proceeds from erroneous judgment more than from depraved feelings; it originates as much in deficiencies of mind as in perversity of heart.

He adds that individualism "saps the virtues of public life" but eventually it attacks all other aspects of public life and degenerates into selfishness. In America, the lack of a sense of the public good is responsible for many problems.

Le Bon's *The Crowd* is a classic work that is remarkable in how it anticipates so much that has occurred in American politics, and in politics in many other countries where "strong men" figures have taken control of countries that were once democracies and have been turned into autocracies. We now recognize that democracy is very fragile and easily damaged or destroyed. There is,

Figure 2.7 Alexis de Tocqueville.

I should add, a question about the way I have characterized Le Bon's thought, as predictive, which is raised in the introduction to *The Crowd*, by Robert Merton.

Robert Merton's "The Ambivalences of Le Bon's *The Crowd*"

Robert Merton (1910–2003) was a famous American sociologist and is considered one of the most important American sociologists. Wikipedia offers this description of his life and accomplishments:

> **Robert King Merton** (born **Meyer Robert Schkolnick**; July 4, 1910 – February 23, 2003) was an American sociologist who is considered a founding father of modern sociology, and a major contributor to the subfield of criminology. He spent most of his career teaching at Columbia University, where he attained the rank of University Professor. In 1994 he was awarded the National Medal of Science for his contributions to the field and for having founded the sociology of science.[1][i]
>
> Merton developed notable concepts, such as "unintended consequences", the "reference group", and "role strain", but is perhaps best known for the terms "role model" and "self-fulfilling prophecy".[2] The concept of *self-fulfilling prophecy*, which is a central element in modern sociological, political, and economic theory, is one type of process through which a belief or expectation affects the outcome of a situation or the way a person or group will behave.[3][4] More specifically, as Merton defined, "the self-fulfilling prophecy is, in the beginning, a false definition of the situation evoking a new behavior, which makes the originally false conception come true".[5]

(https://en.wikipedia.org/wiki/Robert_K._Merton)

Merton's concept of the "role model" first appeared in a study of the socialization of medical students at Columbia University. The term grew from his theory of the *reference group*, the group to which individuals compare themselves but to which they do not necessarily belong. Social roles were central to Merton's theory of *social groups*. Merton emphasized that, rather than a person assuming just one role and one status, they have a status set in the social structure that has, attached to it, a whole set of expected behaviors. I will discuss some of the more important points he makes in his introduction to *The Crowd*. Merton starts his introduction to *The Crowd* by quoting Gordon W. Allport, one of the most important social psychologists, who suggested that Le Bon's book is "perhaps the most influential book ever written in social psychology." Merton says that whether or not Allport was correct, *The Crowd* has exerted a powerful influence on the field of social psychology.

He mentions the topics Le Bon deals with (1960: vii):

> Social conformity and over conformity, the leveling of taste, the revolt of the masses, popular culture, the other-directed self, mass movements, the self-alienation of man, the process of bureaucratization, the escape from freedom into the arms of a Leader, and the role of the unconscious in social behavior.

LeBon's interest in the unconscious attracted the attention of Sigmund Freud, who, in his book on group psychology, wrote about Le Bon's work. Merton explains (1960: ix):

> Le Bon spotted the "fundamental" fact of group psychology by dwelling on the "intensification of the emotions" and the "inhibition of the intellect." *But*, says Freud, he did not see the explanation in the psychological processes that establish emotional ties between the members of groups.

Merton mentions another matter that Le Bon did not deal with relative to the matter of leveling in crowds (1960: xi):

> Le Bon saw and emphasized the tendency toward "leveling" in the crowd, the demand for full equality on the depressed level of mediocrity. *But*, in Freud's judgment, he did not see that this was the outward and visible result of an underlying process in which crowd members "identify themselves with one another by means of a similar love for some object," the "object," in Freud's technical vocabulary, being in this instance the leader.

He is focused on problem-finding and not problem-solving, which suggests Le Bon's focus was somewhat limited, even though he discussed many topics. Le Bon, Merton writes, reflected the climate of opinion or cultural atmosphere at the time he wrote *The Crowd*. As Merton explains (1960: xxxi):

> His is the method of social philosophers, social psychologists, and social observers, prevalent in his own day and far from absent in ours:

the method of using historical anecdotes as a source of ideas and the illusion that the source somehow authenticates the interpretation stemming from them.

Then Merton suggests there is a prophetic element in Le Bon's work (1960: xxxiii):

> Reasonably prophetic…is Le Bon's image of crowd-man as progressively engulfed in popular culture that installs mediocrity and vulgarity as the measure of top-most worth. And his portrait of crowd-man as one peculiarly susceptible to the judgments and tastes of others.

Le Bon was a physician and not a trained social scientist and so he never learned how to assemble and analyze sociological data methodically in order to determine whether or not his ideas were correct. For Merton, Le Bon's book is of uneven quality, based on inferences from his observations. As Merton puts it (1960: xxxvii):

> It is full of ideas: some of whose sound and fruitful; some sound but still to bear fruit; some decidedly unsound but provocative of other ideas that have proved valid; and finally, some in the unhappy condition of being both unsound and fruitless.

Merton concludes his introduction with an appraisal of Le Bon's contribution to social psychology (1960: xxxix):

> A vogue book, repeatedly germane to Le Bon's time and ours, never entirely new nor strictly true but in composite endlessly perceptive, better at its best and worse at its worst than any author had any way of knowing, written between the lines as much as in them, alternatively provincial and backward-looking, using history effectively in practice while rejecting its truth and utility in principle, crystallizing into uniformities of human behavior the dramatic events of his time that exhibited these uniformities, and cluttered with ideological curiosities that do not affects its substance, Le Bon's *The Crowd* is still a book worth reading.

Robert D. Kaplan, the chair of geopolitics at the Foreign Policy Research Institute, wrote an article, *The Tyranny of the 21st-Century Crowd*, that appeared in the October 8, 2021 issue of *The Wall Street Journal*. He discusses a work by Elias Canetti, *Crowds and Power*, in which Canetti describes how the crowd (2021: A27):

> EMERGES from the need of the lonely individual to conform with others. Because he can't exert dominance on his own, he exerts it through a crowd that speaks with one voice....The crowd sees itself as entirely pure, having attained the highest virtue. Thus, one aim of the crowd is to hunt down the insufficiently virtuous. The tyranny of the crowd has many aspects but Canetti says its most blatant form is that of the "questioner," and the accuser.

Kaplan discusses the difference between the twentieth century, which was an age of mass communication where ideology was delivered from the top down, and the twenty-first century where digital networks enable ideology to be delivered from the bottom up. But the goals of each are the same and so are the results (2021: A27):

> The intimidation of dissent through a professed monopoly on virtue. If you don't agree with us, you are not only wrong but morally wanting, and as such should not only be denounced but destroyed.... The lust for purity combined with the tyranny of social-media technology in the hands of the young—who have little sense of the past and of tradition—threatens to create an era of the most fearsome mobs in history.

I would question whether Kaplan is correct about the young and suggest his comments apply more directly, in America, to the middle-aged who form the audience for Trump's rallies and his Twitter and Facebook commentaries before he was banned from them for spreading misinformation and lies. But Kaplan was correct about social media helping create fearsome mobs—as the attack on the Capitol building on January 6, 2021, demonstrated. He concludes his article by saying that the direction of history cannot be known and that it is important to fight on—in support of liberal democracy, one must assume.

Leon Bramson, a sociologist, discusses Le Bon and other writers about crowds at the turn of the century in his book, *The Political Context of Sociology*. He writes (1961: 53):

> To an unsophisticated eye these studies would appear to have come from nowhere. But this is not the case: they are usually inspired by

anti-democratic sentiments, and appear to be aimed at discrediting not only the lower orders, with their claim for increased political power through the general franchise, but also in some cases the whole liberal scheme of parliamentarianism…. The characteristics of "crowds" described by these writers comprise for the most part a catalogue of ugliness and brutality, blind emotion and suggestibility, stupidity and intolerance.

These writers, Bramson says, had aristocratic tendencies and looked down on the common man and woman and the liberal politicians seeking to empower them politically. The writers about crowds often compared people in crowds with children and savages, both incapable of self-governing.

Bramson quotes Gordon Allport, a psychologist, who argues that physical proximity is unnecessary for people to be in a crowd (1961: 55):

Thousands of isolated individuals may acquire, at certain moments, and under the influence of violent emotions,—such as for example of a great national event—the characteristics of a psychological crowd.

This is an important point that has relevance to our understanding of crowd behavior. Members of a crowd don't have to be in the same place, but can be scattered all over the country. Bramson makes an assertion about crowds in America that is questionable and will be discussed in my chapter on national character and crowds (1961: 33):

Lacking a feudal tradition…and possessing from the beginning a liberal-democratic condition, the United States does not provide fertile soil for the development of an anti-democratic social psychology of crowds…. There is almost nothing in the nature of published material in American social psychology and sociology in the 20th century which reflects the passionate interest in crowds on the part of these conservatives who wrote during the last decade of the 19th.

He suggests that American academics became interested in a variant of crowd behavior, namely, collective behavior and mass behavior, leading to investigations of mass culture and popular culture which is different in many respects from studies of crowd behavior.

Were Bramson to watch American television during the past five years, I suspect he would have changed his ideas about America not being a place where crowds were important. We used to say "It couldn't happen here" about fascism, but now, I suggest, many people have changed their minds on that matter. In the next chapter, we will find that one of Le Bon's readers, Sigmund Freud, thought *The Crowd* was definitely worth reading. Freud also had many important things to say about psychology and crowds.

Group Psychology and the Analysis of the Ego (German: *Massenpsychologie und Ich-Analyse*) is a 1921 book by Sigmund Freud, the founder of psychoanalysis. In this monograph, Freud describes psychological mechanisms at work within mass movements. A *mass*, according to Freud, is a "temporary entity, consisting of heterogeneous elements that have joined together for a moment."[1] He refers heavily to the writings of sociologist and psychologist Gustave Le Bon (1841–1931), summarizing his work at the beginning of the book in the chapter *Le Bon's Schilderung der Massenseele* ("Le Bon's description of the group mind"). Like Le Bon, Freud says that as part of the mass, the individual acquires a sense of infinite power that allows him to act on impulses that he would otherwise have to curb as an isolated individual. These feelings of power and security allow the individual not only to act as part of the mass but also to feel safety in numbers. This is accompanied, however, by a loss of conscious personality and a tendency of the individual to be infected by any emotion within the mass, and to amplify the emotion, in turn, by "mutual induction." Overall, the mass is "impulsive, changeable, and irritable. It is controlled almost exclusively by the unconscious."[2]

Freud distinguishes between two types of masses. One is the short-lived kind, characterized by a rapidly transient interest, such as trends. The other kind consists of more permanent and enduring masses, which are highly organized, such as the Church or the military. "The masses of the former type, so to speak, ride on the latter, like the short but high waves on the long swell of the sea."[3] However, the same basic mental processes operate in both kinds of masses.

Freud refers back to his theory of instincts and believes that masses are held together by libidinal bonds. Each individual in the mass acts on impulses of love that are diverted from their original objectives. They pursue no direct sexual goal, but "do not therefore work less vigorously."

https://en.wikipedia.org/w

Chapter 3

GROUP PSYCHOLOGY AND THE ANALYSIS OF THE EGO

Freud wrote his book in 1921, many years after the publication of Le Bon's *The Crowd*. Freud commented on the book in his work on group psychology since they were both, in many respects, writing about the same topic. The chapters in Freud's book are the following:

Freud begins his book, in his introduction, by explaining that individual psychology and group psychology are really two sides of the same coin (Figure 3.1). He explains that the mental health of individuals is almost always connected to others so that individual psychology is also, at the same time, social or group psychology.

Group psychology, he adds, deals with individuals as they are members of some component of a group, such as a race, a caste, a nation, an institution, or of a crowd of people organized for a particular purpose into a group. This leads him to a discussion of Le Bon and his notion of the group mind.

Figure 3.1 Sigmund Freud.

Freud asks three questions we must consider when dealing with group psychology (1922:3):

1. What is a group?
2. How does it exercise a decisive influence over the mental life of individuals?
3. What is the nature of the change it forces on individuals?

He mentions Le Bon's ideas about individuals in groups being affected by contagion and heightened suggestibility but does not recognize, Freud points out, that contagion is best understood as a manifestation of suggestibility. He adds that all the features of groups that Le Bon discusses can be explained by psychoanalysts: the fact that in groups people lose their individual inhibitions, demand illusions, and are as strongly influenced by what is false as what is true. After dealing with Le Bon's ideas, and saying its emphasis on unconscious aspects of mental life fits in with his thinking, Freud moves on to the theories of a psychologist, William McDougall, who wrote a book *The Group Mind,* that was published in 1920 and emphasizes the role of emotions in people in groups who behave like unruly children.

Freud discusses McDougall's ideas about dealing with the problems of groups by procuring for their members the characteristics of individuals, which membership in groups extinguish. This involves individuals recognizing their continuity, becoming aware of their self-consciousness, their traditions and customs, and associating with other groups.

This leads to Freud's discussion of "Suggestion and Libido" in which he deals with the intensification of emotions and inhibiting the intellect of people in groups, or, in more general terms, the mental change individuals experience in groups. He argues that love relationships, also to be understood as emotional ties are the essence of the group mind.

Freud offers as examples two highly organized, lasting groups: the Church and the Army, in which there is a leader or head who loves all members of the group. As Freud explains (1921:15)

> It is to be noticed that in these two artificial groups each individual is bound by libidinal ties on the one hand to the leader (Christ, the Commander-in-Chief) and on the other hand to the other members of the group. How these two ties are related to each other, whether they are of the same kind and the same value, and how they are to be described psychologically—these questions must be reserved for subsequent enquiry [...] It would appear as though we were on the right road towards an explanation of the principal phenomenon of group psychology—the individual's lack of freedom in a group. If each individual is bound in two directions by such an intense emotional tie, we shall find no difficulty in attributing to that circumstance the alteration and limitation which have been observed in his personality.

Freud argues that intimate emotional relations between two people always generate feelings of aversion and hostility that are eliminated by repression and he says the same thing happens to people in groups. Eventually, people bond because of the libidinal ties they have with others in their groups. He suggests that identification, the earliest emotion, which ties people with others, is found in the feeling children have for their parents and is also found in the relations the members of groups have with their leaders. This eventually takes the form of love, but in a complicated manner (1923:23):

> In connection with this question of being in love we have always been struck by the phenomenon of sexual overvaluation—the fact that the loved object enjoys a certain amount of freedom from criticism, and that all its characteristics are valued more highly than those of people who are not loved, or than its own were at a time when it itself was not loved. If the sensual impulses are more or less effectively repressed or set aside, the illusion is produced that the object has come to be sensually loved on account of its spiritual merits, whereas on the contrary these merits may really only have been lent to it by its sensual charm. The tendency which falsifies judgement in this respect is that of idealization

What happens, Freud maintains, is that the object of our love, the leader, has replaced the individual ego ideal. This is connected with the regression of our mental activity to our earliest days, a phenomenon found in children and among savages. Freud says that the behavior we find in groups is not just a matter of gregariousness, the sense that individuals feel incomplete without others. The herd instinct, he points out, is not adequate because it doesn't leave room for a leader, who becomes just another member of the herd. Instead, Freud writes, the regression of groups seems to suggest the revival of what he calls the primal horde, which means groups exhibit the characteristics of the earliest group known to man. He ends the book (except for the postscript) by dealing with the relationship between the ego and the ego ideal (1923:32):

> We are aware that what we have been able to contribute towards the explanation of the libidinal structure of groups leads back to the distinction between the ego and the ego ideal and to the double kind of tie which this makes possible—identification, and putting the object in the place of the ego ideal. The assumption of this kind of differentiating grade in the ego as a first step in an analysis of the ego must gradually establish its justification in the most various regions of psychology.

The ego, let us remember, is that element of the psyche that mediates between the demands of the superego (in essence, guilt) and the id (in essence, lust and desire). When the ego ideal replaces the ego, individuals lose the capacity to reason and become subject to the desires of their ego ideal. The ego, the id, and the superego are part of Freud's structural hypothesis about mental functioning. Charles Brenner offers the following description of these three entities (1974:38):

> We may say that the id comprises the psychic representatives of the drives, the ego consists of those functions which have to do with the individual's relation to his environment, and the superego comprises the moral precepts of our minds as well as our ideal aspirations. The drives, of course, we assume to be present from birth, but the same is certainly not true of interest in or control of the environment on the one hand, nor of any moral sense or aspirations on the other. It is obvious that neither of the latter, that is neither the ego nor the superego, develops till sometime after birth. Freud expressed this fact by assuming that the id comprised the entire psychic apparatus at birth and that the ego and superego were originally parts of the id which differentiated sufficiently in the course of growth to warrant they're being considered as separate functional entities. (p. 38)

These entities—the id, ego, and superego—are extremely complicated, and Freud and other theorists have written at great length about how each develops and functions, and the importance of each to the individual's psychic life. In his postscript, Freud discusses his theory about the myth of the father and the primal horde in which individuals band together and kill the father and renounce his heritage. This myth, Freud explains, helps individuals emerge from their group consciousness. It is reasonable to suggest that Trump can be seen, at the unconscious level, as a father figure and the ego ideal of his many followers and that they have, to a considerable degree, collectively abandoned their individual or personal egos and their rational capacities because of their powerful and irrational identification with Trump.

Many Americans watched Trump on *The Apprentice* and developed a parasocial identification with him, which means they thought they knew him very well. Wikipedia defines parasocial interactions as follows:

> **Parasocial interaction** (**PSI**) refers to a kind of psychological relationship experienced by an audience in their mediated encounters with performers in the mass media, particularly on television and on online platforms. Viewers or listeners come to consider media personalities as friends, despite having no or limited interactions with them. PSI is described as an illusionary experience, such that media audiences interact with personas (e.g., talk show hosts, celebrities, fictional characters, social media influencers) as if they are engaged in a reciprocal relationship with them. The term was coined by Donald Horton and Richard Wohl in 1956.
>
> https://en.wikipedia.org/wiki/Parasocial_interaction

Whether the mob members are also cult members is the subject of my next chapter, on crowds and cults (Figure 3.2).

Figure 3.2 January 6, 2021, Riot at the Capitol. Photo was taken from television.

In modern English, a **cult** is a social group that is defined by its unusual religious, spiritual, or philosophical beliefs, or by its common interest in a particular personality, object, or goal. This sense of the term is controversial, having divergent definitions in both popular culture and academia, and has also been an ongoing source of contention among scholars across several fields of study. The word "cult" is usually considered pejorative.

An older sense of the word *cult* involves a set of religious devotional practices that are conventional within their culture, are related to a particular figure, and are often associated with a particular place. References to the "cult" of a particular Catholic saint, or the imperial cult of ancient Rome, for example, use this sense of the word.

While the literal and original sense of the word remains in use in the English language, a derived sense of "excessive devotion" arose in the nineteenth century.[i] Beginning in the 1930s, cults became the object of sociological study in the context of the study of religious behavior.[4] Since the 1940s, the Christian countercult movement has opposed some sects and new religious movements, labeling them "cults" because of their unorthodox beliefs. Since the 1970s, the secular anti-cult movement has opposed certain groups, and in reaction to acts of violence which have been committed by some of their members, it has frequently charged them with practicing mind control. Scholars and the media have disputed some of the claims and actions of anti-cult movements, leading to further public controversy.

Sociological classifications of religious movements may identify a cult as a social group with socially deviant or novel beliefs and practices,[5] although this is often unclear. Other researchers present a less-organized picture of cults, saying that they arise spontaneously around novel beliefs and practices. Groups labelled as "cults" range in size from local groups with a few followers to international organizations with millions of adherents.

https://en.wikipedia.org/wiki/Cult

Chapter 4

CROWDS AND CULTS

We have already explored, indirectly, what cults are, from Le Bon's social-psychology perspective and Freud's analytic perspective. The question I wish to resolve here is: how does a crowd become a cult? We might also ask whether all crowds eventually become cults.

Your Dictionary on the Internet offers this definition of a cult:

> The definition of a cult is a group of people with extreme dedication to a certain leader or set of beliefs that are often viewed as odd by others, or is an excessive and misplaced admiration for someone or something, or is something that is popular among a certain segment of society. People who follow a creepy, pseudo-religious leader who makes them believe that their salvation lies in giving him money are an example of a cult.

Cult Meaning: Best Ten Definitions of Cult (yourdictionary.com)

This definition, with its focus on raising money, seems particularly apt when it comes to dealing with Donald Trump as a cult leader and world-class grifter. Freud talked about the significance of the erotic feelings people in crowds have for each other and their leaders, and the epigraph mentions the religious aspects of cults, so it is not too difficult to see the erotic feelings people in crowds have merging into religious attitudes. A review of a book about Trump as a cult leader by Steven Hassan offers some insights into the relationship between Trump and his followers:

> Since the 2016 election, Donald Trump's behavior has become both more disturbing and yet increasingly familiar. He relies on phrases like, "fake news," "build the wall," and continues to spread the divisive mentality of us-vs.-them. He lies constantly, has no conscience, never admits when he is wrong, and projects all of his shortcomings onto others. He has become more authoritarian, more outrageous, and yet

many of his followers remain blindly devoted. Scott Adams, the creator of Dilbert and a major Trump supporter, calls him one of the most persuasive people living. His need to squash alternate information and his insistence on constant ego-stroking are all characteristics of other famous leaders—*cult* leaders.

In *The Cult of Trump*, mind control and licensed mental health expert Steven Hassan draws parallels between our current president and people like Jim Jones, David Koresh, Ron Hubbard, and Sun Myung Moon, arguing that this presidency is in many ways like a destructive cult. He specifically details the ways in which people are influenced through an array of social psychology methods and how they become fiercely loyal and obedient. Hassan was a former "Moonie" himself, and he presents a "thoughtful and well-researched analysis of some of the most puzzling aspects of the current presidency, including the remarkable passivity of fellow Republicans [and] the gross pandering of many members of the press" (Thomas G. Gutheil, MD and professor of psychiatry, Harvard Medical School). *The Cult of Trump* is an accessible and in-depth analysis of the president, showing that under the right circumstances, even sane, rational, well-adjusted people can be persuaded to believe the most outrageous ideas. "This book is a must for anyone who wants to understand the current political climate" (Judith Stevens-Long, Ph.D. and author of *Living Well, Dying Well*).

https://www.amazon.com/dp/B082J593ZQ/ref=dp-kindle-redirect?_encoding=UTF8&btkr=1

If Hassan is correct, Trump is best understood as the leader of a cult of Republican voters and Republican members of Congress who do not recognize that they are members of his cult. The politicians see him as a means of avoiding getting primaried in their elections and of gaining votes from his "base" of admirers, and die-hard followers, who see him in religious terms in terms of their affection for him and his values.

Trump is a narcissist, and that plays a role in his position as a cult leader, according to Elena Sada, in an article posted January 19, 2021, on the Internet. She was, for a time, a member of a cult and so her article is based on her experiences:

When I was in Regnum Christi, which was considered a cult led by abusive narcissist Marcial Maciel LC, a Catholic priest who managed to gain the favors of John Paul II and establish a religious order, I often asked the question: why did some of us became enablers and codependents within the group, while others were simply victims of the founder's lies? I came to the conclusion that it depended on the person's degree of involvement and their level of leadership in the group. While cult *lower-ranking* leaders do not always commit crimes, their guilt relies on the dissemination of lies, even when they believed them to be true – in which case is the result of ignorance by omission; cult to personality blinded them and led others blindly.

Trump followers idealize Trump in virtue of the faith and codependency they have developed toward the local or social-media leaders who have convinced them that mainstream media, and mainstream everything, are attacking them and slandering their ideals. As a consequence, they have become more determined to stand by, and defend, the *principles* that they believe are superior and in danger, and defend the leader who is supposed to guarantee those principles.

https://ctmirror.org/category/ct-viewpoints/is-trump-leading-a-cult/

Generally speaking, members of cults recognize that they belong to a cult but in Trump's case, I would suggest that most members of Trump's cult are unaware of their involvement in his cult. Trump holds countless rallies in which he repeats his assertions and convinces those attending that their beliefs and values are the correct ones and that he is engaged in a heroic battle against his foes. Some members of his cult also belong to QAnon, a bizarre cult that claims that democratic politicians are pederasts and drink the blood of the children they abduct. During the beginning of the 2016 presidential campaign, many members of the Republican Party called him a "con" artist and said many uncomplimentary things about him, only to reverse themselves when he was, to everyone's surprise, elected. Many Republican politicians blamed him for causing the insurrection of January 6, 2021—only to reverse themselves because they feared his base, his cult followers, would attack them in their primaries. In an interview in *Vanity Fair,* Steven Hassan offers his perspectives on the Trump Cult. The article was titled:

SO MANY GREAT, EDUCATED, FUNCTIONAL PEOPLE WERE BRAINWASHED": CAN TRUMP'S CULT OF FOLLOWERS BE DEPROGRAMMED?

My thoughts about cults are that you can have a cult that's benign or even positive, or you can have a destructive authoritarian cult. When I talk about the cult of Trump, I'm talking about a destructive authoritarian cult. This is defined by four overlapping components that I referred to as the BITE model of authoritarian control.

The *b* of BITE stands for behavior control. Then the *i* is information control. Thought control is the *t*, and *e* is emotional control. My definition of an authoritarian cult is these four components are used to change the person into a mirror or a clone of the cult, that is dependent and obedient. As a mental health professional, we think of that as a dissociative disorder. Where the person's real self is still there, it's just suppressed. This new identity has taken over, and thought-stopping mechanisms and phobias are installed in the cult identity to keep it in control.

(https://www.vanityfair.com/news/2021/01/can-trumps-cult-of-followers-be-deprogrammed)

So we have four hallmarks of destructive authoritarian cults:

1. Behavior control
2. Information control
3. Thought control
4. Emotional control.

It is by asserting these different kinds of control that crowds become cults. As Le Bon suggested, people in crowds give up much of their autonomy, and their intellectual level becomes depleted. Thus, crowds are, by nature, fertile grounds for their leaders to turn them into cults.

Hassan offers a chilling description of how Trump was able to assert control over the Republican members of Congress, many of whom are lawyers and most are highly educated. There have been many books on the pathological nature of Trump's psyche, and the general consensus by psychologists and psychoanalysts (including his niece) is that he is a malignant narcissist who is quite likely unaware of what a damaged individual he is. In this respect, he is like many cult leaders.

We might wonder whether cults tend to attract people with certain psychological problems that make them more susceptible to cults. Research I've conducted suggests that anyone can be "sucked into" joining a cult, but it would seem some kinds of people are more prone to join cults than others. Here is a list of the types of people most open to becoming members of cults. I am not talking about intelligence here but personality factors.

Cults Tend to Be Full of People Who Are:

Isolated

In the cult, they find fellowship but at a terrible price—the loss of their independence and, most times, a depreciation of their rational sensibilities.

Le Bon talked about the diminution of rationality by people in crowds and the same applies to people in cults. Sometimes, a crowd is a cult or becomes a cult, though members of the cult don't recognize this has happened.

Alienated

It is easy to understand how people who are alienated from others join cults, seeking a means of escaping from their feelings of loneliness and separation from others and themselves.

Feel Marginal

People who are loners and feel marginal, on the side of things, without a group to give them a sense of identity and status, are more likely to join cults than people who have strong group affiliations, such as memberships in religious organizations and social groups that make them feel wanted and important.

Insecure

Everyone suffers from a degree of insecurity, but people who feel terribly insecure join cults because being a member of a cult provides security, but at a terrible cost: usually a loss of personal identity and victimization by the mind control techniques of the leaders of cults.

Suffering from a Sense of Relative Deprivation

Everyone recognizes that some people have more money and better life chances than others, but if people have a decent amount of wealth and can enjoy some minor extravagances, they do not become jealous of those who are much richer than they are. The American Dream teaches us that anyone can succeed if they are willing to work hard enough, so people who don't think they are successful believe that eventually, they will find a way to be successful. When they lose faith in the American Dream and decide that they are more or less going to be stuck in the socioeconomic class to which they belong, then feelings of relative deprivation become powerful and can lead to joining cults, which promise all kinds of benefits to their members.

Angry

If you add up the various topics I have been discussing, they can lead, in some people, to powerful feelings of anger at others (especially elites who supposedly look down on them), at the makeup of the societies in which they live, and at the politicians in their cities, states, and the country. This anger takes the form of being resentful of others and seeking solace in a cult, which promises them relief from their feelings of anger and resentment, the promise of arcane knowledge leading to insights into life that will benefit them. Many cults are utopian in theory and dystopic in reality. Frequently, cult members are exploited sexually and financially.

Anomic

The term "anomie" means no norms. The term was introduced by the French sociologist Emile Durkheim. In societies where there are few norms and people feel lost and unsure of how to behave, cults offer security and the experience of belonging to an organization with many rules. Trump is anomic, with no regard for conventions or expectations regarding the behavior of normally socialized leaders.

Grid-Group Theory and Cults

Grid-Group Theory was developed by the English social anthropologist Mary Douglas, who collaborated with the American political scientist Aaron Wildavsky on several projects.

In *Cultural Theory*, written by Michael Thompson, Richard Ellis, and Aaron Wildavsky, we find a description of Grid-Group Theory (1990:5):

> Our theory has a specific point of departure: the grid-group typology proposed by Mary Douglas. She argues that the variability of an individual's involvement with social life can be adequately captured by two dimensions of sociality: group and grid. *Group* refers to the extent to which an individual is incorporated in bounded units. The greater the incorporation, the more the individual is subject to group determination. *Grid* denotes to the degree to which an individual's life is circumscribed by externally imposed prescriptions. The more binding and extensive the scope of the prescriptions, the less of life that is open to individual negotiation.

Grid-Group Theory argues that our behavior is shaped by two different forces: one is the strength of the groups to which we belong (and the amount of control they have over us) and the other is the number of rules and prescriptions to which we are subject. The group boundaries can be very strong or relatively weak and the number of rules and prescriptions can be few in number or numerous. For example, Catholic priests have strong group boundaries and many rules, while Reform rabbis have weaker group boundaries and fewer rules. Soldiers in the United States Army and other military branches have strong boundaries and many rules. Armies are hierarchical, with a very strong and elaborated chain of command. People who belong to sports clubs have weak group boundaries and few rules. It is not difficult to join them and they don't have many rules. Wildavsky (1982) explained in "Conditions for a Pluralist Democracy or Cultural Pluralism Means More Than One Political Culture in a Country" (1982:7):

> What matters to people is how they should live with other people. The great questions of social life are "Who am I?" (To what kind of a group do I belong?) and What should I do? (Are there many or few prescriptions I am expected to obey?). Groups are strong or weak according to whether they have boundaries separating them from others. Decisions are taken either for the group as a whole (strong boundaries) or for individuals or families (weak boundaries). Prescriptions are few or many indicating the individual internalizes a large or a small number of behavioral norms to which he or she is bound. By combining boundaries with prescriptions [...] the most general answers to the questions of social life can be combined to form four different political cultures,

In Table 4.1, I take these two dimensions, Grid and Group, and show how they lead to four different lifestyles depending on the strength or weakness of the group boundaries and number of rules and prescriptions. The names for the lifestyles I have used here were used by Aaron Wildavsky in his work on political cultures; Mary Douglas had different names for Egalitarians and Fatalists: Enclavists and Isolates.

Table 4.1 Four Lifestyles.

Group Boundaries	Strength of Rules	Number of Rules
Hierarchical Elitists	Strong	Many
Egalitarians	Strong	Few
Individualists	Weak	Few
Fatalists	Weak	Many

Wildavsky explained how these groups are formed. He writes (quoted in A. A. Berger, 1990:6):

Strong groups with numerous prescriptions that vary with social roles combine to form hierarchical collectivism. Strong groups whose members follow few prescriptions form an egalitarian culture, a shared life of voluntary consent, without coercion or inequality. Competitive individualism joins few prescriptions with weak boundaries, thereby encouraging ever new combinations. When groups are weak and prescriptions strong, so that decisions are made for them by people on the outside, the controlled culture is fatalistic.

Grid-Group Theory tells us that cults are hierarchical in nature with strong boundaries and many rules made by the leader of the cult. Cults are not egalitarian and are not full of individualists who want to do things their way.

Mary Douglas describes the importance of lifestyles in an article she wrote "In Defence of Shopping, found in Pasi Falk and Colin Campbell's *The Shopping Experience*" (1997:17–18):

We have to make a radical shift away from thinking about consumption as a manifestation of individual choices. Culture itself is the result of myriads of individual choices, not primarily between commodities but between kinds of relationships. The basic choice that a rational individual has to make is the choice about what kind of society to live in. According to that choice, the rest follows. Artefacts are selected to demonstrate the choice. Food is eaten, clothes are worn, books, music, holidays, all the rest are choices that conform with the original choice for a form of society. Commodities are chosen because they are not neutral; they are chosen because they would not be tolerated in the rejected forms of society and are therefore permissible in the preferred form. Hostility is implicit in their selection [...]

When she writes about the basic choice people have to make about "what kind of society to live in," she is dealing with which lifestyle people choose. The lifestyle people in cults choose is a perverted variation of the elitist lifestyle, and like all lifestyles, it conflicts with all other lifestyles (Figure 4.1).

Figure 4.1 Mary Douglas.

The Nine Personality Traits of People Likely to Join a Cult

An article in *Bustle*, an online American women's magazine, discusses the personality traits of people likely to join cults:

> If you are wondering who joins cults and why, the short, but creepy answer is that pretty much anyone can get sucked into them. "That is the insidiousness of mind-manipulation," Lisa Kohn, a cult survivor and author of the upcoming memoir *To the Moon and Back*, tells *Bustle*. "Nearly anyone can be manipulated by the promise of a better tomorrow or the answers to their questions or a sense of their inherent rightness (or sinfulness)." But there do seem to be a few personality traits that can make someone more likely to join a cult, that these organizations (for lack of a better word) often play into.

Depending on someone's personality and what they're seeking in life, they may be a bit more susceptible to what a cult promises. "Cults prey on vulnerability [...] to facilitate their cause," psychologist Dr. Michele Barton, director of Psychology Life Well, tells *Bustle*. "Cults seek out the disenfranchised and outcasts. People most in need of support are lured in by the prospect of belonging somewhere or to something meaningful."

And that's why cults can seem so great, at first, as well as why it can be difficult for people to realize they're even joining one. As Kohn says, "Every right-minded person would most likely say, 'I am not susceptible to a cult.' And every person I know and knew who was in a cult would tell you that they were not in a cult." But again, this is all part of the brain-washing. "Once you're in, you know it's right, and therefore it's not a cult," Kohn says.

The article then lists the personality types that cults search for when looking for recruits:

Those Who Want To Feel Validated

People with many unmet approval needs see a cult as a welcoming group that makes them feel good about themselves, according to psychologist and executive coach Dr. Perpetua Neo tells *Bustle*. Cult members tend to play into this trait when they're out seeking new members.

Those Who Are Seeking An Identity

For those with an identity that is not stable, who are not sure of who they are, then a cult makes things simple, according to Dr. Neo. For people who are drifting through life or don't feel that they have any relationships that are deep enough and are lonely, a cult may provide that sense of family that they may never have experienced.

Those Who Are Followers, Not Leaders

Cults are often centered on a strong leader, who is typically dynamic and warm and inspiring—all traits that can be incredibly attractive to someone whose personality lends itself to following others, instead of being a leader themselves.

Those Who Are Seeking Meaning

We all want to figure out the "meaning of life," find our purpose, and learn more about ourselves. But people who are desperate seekers of truth may be more likely to get caught up in a group that offers quick answers to their questions, or promises a future that seems more meaningful and bright "Cults, with simplistic explanations coupled with a charismatic leader who has perfected the modus operandi to manipulate you, play on this," Dr. Neo says. "If what they offer aligns with your desire for meaning, then you become likelier to join them."

Those Who Have Schizotypal Thinking

Schizotypal thinkers walk along the edge of schizophrenia, without actually having the delusions or disconnection from society that's associated with the disorder, Dr. Neo says. They do, however, have odd beliefs and behaviors that might fall into the realm of conspiracy-type or alien-type or supernatural-type beliefs.

Those Who Are Highly Suggestible

Cults work by brainwashing their members. So really, anyone can get sucked in or fall victim to their mind games. But this may be even more likely for someone who tends to be highly suggestible or gullible, as well as anyone who wants to find meaning in life so desperately they're willing to give *anything* a go.

Those Who Constantly Blame Others

People who do not wish to take personal responsibility for their actions, and prefer to defer to a higher power to account for their own behavior, are more likely to join a cult. Blamers make perfect cult members since they are good at following others and have no moral issues about doing so, regardless of what happens.

Those Who Are Always Angry

People who are always angry or discontented are more susceptible to cults or other extremist groups because the extremist group or cult provides them with a sense of belonging, and being right about things. Humans are social animals with a strong need to belong to something and when do not have that feeling, they can find that belonging in cults and extremist political groups.

Those Who Have Very Low Self-Worth

Cults prey on loners, people who feel like outsiders, so it is easy to see why low self-worth may make someone more likely to get swept up in a group that makes them feel like they belong to an entity larger than themselves.

This list is useful because it offers us a picture of the kinds of persons likely to become members of cults and describes their emotional needs and psychological problems they face. Not everyone who has one or more of these traits becomes a member of a cult, but people with these needs are the most likely to join a cult.

Google Search on Trump as the Leader of a Cult

We might ask whether these traits can be found in Trump's base and many members of the Republican Party. A search on Google for "Trump as the Leader of a Cult" led to 27,750,000 results. (Accessed 10/12/2021.) The first results on the Google site follow:

A Leading Cult Expert Explains How the President Uses Mind
https://www.amazon.com › Cult-Trump-Leading-Explains...
Amazon.com: The **Cult** of **Trump**: A Leading **Cult** Expert Explains How the President Uses Mind Control: 9781982127336: Hassan, Steven: Books.
Jan 19, 2021 — My experience as a former **cult** member and researcher in the field of Social Sciences earned me the ability to identify narcissism and...
Congresswoman Shot At Jonestown Compares Donald Trump...
https://www.forbes.com › markjoyella › 2021/08/01 › c...
Aug 1, 2021 — Jackie Speier (D-Calif.) compared former President Donald **Trump** to the **cult leader** Jim Jones, telling CNN's Brian Stelter that "there is no...
Certified Loser Donald Trump Is Rebranding MAGA as a Full...
https://www.thedailybeast.com › certified-loser-donald-t...
Jul 19, 2021 — As a twice-impeached, one-term historical freak show of a president, his only hope is to turn his movement into a **cult**, worshipping himself.
The Cult of Trump | Book by Steven Hassan - Simon & Schuster
https://www.simonandschuster.com › books › Steven-H...
A masterful and eye-opening examination of **Trump** and the coercive control tactics he uses to build a fanatical devotion in his supporters written by "an ...

Can Trump's Cult of Followers Be Deprogrammed? | Vanity Fair
https://www.vanityfair.com › News › donald trump
Jan 21, 2021—As the president's conspiracy theories start to unspool with
    his departure from office, **cult** expert Steven Hassan, a former Moonie

Because of the way Trump mocked wearing masks, did not support becoming
vaccinated, and politicized every aspect of dealing with the pandemic, the Trump
cult is also, it turns out, a death cult. Most of the people dying from Omicron
in recent months are unvaccinated, and many of them are Republicans.

The basic unit of semiotics is the *sign* defined conceptually as something that stands for something else, and, more technically, as a spoken or written word, a drawn figure, or a material object unified in the mind with a particular cultural concept. The sign is this unity of word-object, known as a *signifier* with a corresponding, culturally prescribed content or meaning, known as a *signified*. Thus our minds attach the word "dog," or the drawn figure of a "dog," as a signifier to the idea of a "dog," that is, a domesticated canine species possessing certain behavioral characteristics. If we came from a culture that did not possess dogs in daily life, however unlikely, we would not know what the signifier "dog" means. [...] When dealing with objects that are signifiers of certain concepts, cultural meanings, or ideologies of belief, we can consider them not only as "signs," but *sign vehicles*. Signifying objects carry meanings with them.

Mark Gottdiener, The *Theming of America: Dreams,
Visions, and Commercial Spaces.*

Since the meaning of a sign depends on the code within which it is situated, codes provide a framework within which signs make sense. Indeed, we cannot grant something the status of a sign if it does not function within a code [...] The conventions of codes represent a social dimension in semiotics: a code is a set of practices familiar to users of the medium operating with a broad cultural framework [...] When studying cultural practices, semioticians treat as signs any objects or actions which have meaning to the members of a cultural group, seeking to identify the rules or conventions of the codes which underlie the production of meaning within that culture.

Daniel Chandler. *Semiotics: The Basics.* London: Routledge.

Chapter 5

THE SEMIOTICS OF CROWDS

People in crowds often dress in a manner to suggest their allegiance to whatever it is that draws them together. For example, if you go to a college football game, you will often find students from the college and fans of the team are wearing the team colors and sometimes tee shirts and sweatshirts with the team colors and the name of the college or the team (Figure 5.1).

Many people are unfamiliar with semiotics so, since this chapter deals with the semiotics of crowds, let me say a few words about the science of semiotics. There are two founding fathers of semiotics, a Swiss linguist Ferdinand de Saussure (Figure 5.2), who wrote a seminal book, *Course in General Linguistics* that was published in 1915, and the American philosopher Charles Sanders Peirce (Figure 5.3), who wrote many books on the subject and who gave the science its name.

Figure 5.1 Baylor football fans at a game.

Figure 5.2 Ferdinand de Saussure.

Figure 5.3 Charles Sanders Peirce.

The term "semiotics" is based on the Greek word for sign, sēmeîon, and semiotics is the science of signs—a sign being anything that can stand for something else, anything that conveys meaning. For example, our facial expressions are signs, our hairstyles are signs, our clothes are signs, and, according to Pierce, everything is a sign.

Peirce said (cited in Sebeok, 1977, page 6), "this universe is perfused with signs, if it is not composed exclusively of signs."

If Peirce is correct and everything is a sign, semiotics becomes the master science since it enables us to interpret signs, so when you learned what words mean, as a little child and when you learned to read, you began your career as a semiotician. Actually, when you were just a few months old, and your parents smiled at you, and you responded to their smiles, you started your career as a semiotician.

Maya Pines describes this process as follows ("How They Know What You Really Mean"), *San Francisco Chronicle*, October 13, 1982):

> Everything we do sends messages about us in a variety of codes, semiologists contend. We are also on the receiving end of innumerable messages encoded in music, gestures, foods, rituals, books, movies, or advertisements. Yet we seldom realize that we have received such messages, and would have trouble explaining the rules under which they operate.

The science of semiotics teaches us how to understand the messages we are sent by others and also to understand better the messages we send about ourselves to others. Most people are not aware of the messages they are sending and how others are interpreting them and they often make mistakes in interpreting the messages—another word for signs—that others are sending to them. David Chandler, in the epigraph, points out that we need to know codes to understand the meaning of signs, and as we grow up, we learn the codes that unlock the meaning of the signs that are all about us. Take football, for example. You have to learn that when officials raise their hands about their heads so they approximate goal posts, semiotically speaking a sign, it means a football team has scored some points (Figure 5.4).

We have to learn the meaning of signs about every aspect of our lives and everyday experiences, but some people, for one reason or another, do not learn how to interpret signs correctly and have problems relating to others and functioning in society.

People in a football stadium or a baseball park are a crowd in the sense that they all have something in common—they are rooting for one of the two teams with whom they identify. With college football teams, they are students

Figure 5.4 Football official indicating points have been scored.

and others connected to the college or fans of the team. Or students from the opposing team's college or fans of that college or its team.

Some ocean cruise ships can carry about 6000 passengers and a crew of about 2000, but though there are many people on the boat, they don't constitute a crowd, because the only thing tying them together is being on the ship. Except at dining times, many of the passengers are separated from one another, which suggests that the number of people together is not the only criterion for deciding on what constitutes a crowd.

People attending sports contests generally have a unifying factor: their support of one of the two contending teams. Football teams often

Figure 5.5 Texas A&M fans on field after historic win.

have many players, but we think of the players not as members of a crowd, or even a small crowd, but as members of a team. Or, in more generic terms, a small group. People attending a football game can get excited and occasionally act as a flash mob. For example, when Texas A&M defeated Alabama in October 2021, the people watching the game—students and fans of Texas A&M—were so delirious with joy that they stormed onto the playing field in the thousands (Figure 5.5). But they lacked many of the features of a crowd, such as not focusing all their attention on a leader who spoke to them.

When it comes to politics, and other kinds of crowds, matters become more complicated.

Trump's Crowds: A Case Study

Trump held over 300 rallies during his campaign for the presidency and after he became president, and the people at these rallies all fit the classic definition of being members of a crowd. Typically, in a Trump rally, he insults many people, lies about many topics, and enjoys being the center of attention—being a narcissist who delights in the attention of others. The people who attend these rallies are "true believers" who come to have their attitudes and prejudices confirmed by Trump. During videos of his rallies, you see people nodding their heads in agreement with things Trump says and high emotion and instability. Many of them are wearing red Make America Great Again (MAGA) hats, signifiers of their attachment to his politics, which is a blend of White Supremacy

Figure 5.6 Red baseball caps as signifiers of Trump followers.

memes, assertions without evidence, blaming others, namely the Democrats, for problems Americans face, and an assertion of victimhood by Trump that resonates with his followers.

In Figure 2.6, taken from television coverage of one of his rallies, we notice many people with signs for the Trump/Pence ticket and one with "Keep America Great."

He is holding his left hand up, greeting the crowd.

In Figure 5.6, we see that many of the people are wearing red baseball "MAGA" hats. For Trump, the size of his crowds is important because large crowds mean, as he sees things, that he is very popular.

Trump often compared the size of his rally crowds with those of Joe Biden, who was not interested in attracting large crowds because of the pandemic. Trump found it hard to believe that since he attracted so many people to his rallies that he could have lost the election and thus, it would seem, convinced himself that he didn't lose but that Biden and the Democrats stole the election. As a narcissist, he could not admit he lost and thus he promulgated the "Big Lie," which his followers quickly accepted, with dire consequences for the American democratic experiment.

Figure 5.7 "Save America" signs.

Figure 5.7 is interesting for several reasons. First, we see some people wearing "Blacks for Trump 2020.com" and a website for Black people to go to who support Trump.

If you consider that Trump has voiced support for racist organizations and is identified as a White Nationalist by many scholars and journalists, you would wonder why any African-Americans or Black people could support him.

The second interesting thing about the image is that it has many signs saying "Save America." The term "save" has religious implications. America must be saved, Trump followers believe, because it has fallen victim to the lies of the Democrats. They are, for Trump's followers, socialists, if not communists, who want to change America into a multiracial country and replace white Americans with people of color who will presumably vote for Democrats.

Salvation has religious implications and many Trump followers see him in religious terms as something approximating the second coming of Christ. An article in *USA Today* on the Internet reads:

> After a rollercoaster convention that at times seemed off the rails, Donald Trump accepted his party's nomination Thursday and delivered a forceful message to Americans: You should be afraid, very afraid, and I alone can save you.

The phrase "I alone can save you" reflects Trump's monumental ego but also suggests he sees himself as a religious figure—a prophetic voice in the wilderness, as do many of his followers, especially evangelical Christians. The fervor of a high percentage of his followers suggests they see him as a god-like person, even though he has been divorced several times and was unfaithful to his wives and lied something like 30,000 times during his presidency, according to *The Washington Post*. Trump courts religious people who approve of his stance against abortion. One of the more famous images of him shows him holding a Bible, upside down, in front of a church in Washington, DC after he had the area in front of the church cleared of protesters.

The Semiotics of Donald J. Trump

Trump, himself, is semiotically interesting. His hairstyle is his most distinguishing feature. It is generally described as a comb-over. Trump is balding but has grown the hair on the side and back of his head long enough to cover over his bald spots, a sign, we might say, of his vanity and his refusing to face reality. Trump's hair is used by political cartoonists to identify him—along with the color of his hair. If you Google "Trump" and click on images, you find hundreds of photos of him, some of which suggest extreme emotionality, anger, hostility, curious contortions of his mouth (that seem porcine), and other unpleasant attributes (Figure 5.8). Books about Trump by people who worked for him at the White House described him as being constantly enraged and screaming at people, a much different picture of him than one we usually get at his rallies.

The images of Trump with distorted features suggest that he is a deeply disturbed person, the result of his upbringing, according to psychologists who

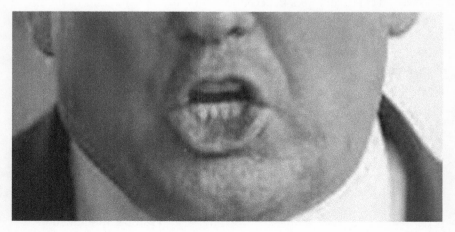

Figure 5.8 Trump's porcine lips.

Figure 5.9 Extreme facial expression of Trump.

have observed his behavior (Figure 5.9). His basic emotion seems to be anger; his typical mood seems to be hostile and irritable; his typical psychological state seems to be impulsivity.

In the past four years, there have been more than a thousand books about Trump in the English language, and more books about him are being published almost every day, so it seems.

Trump's crowds see in him the personification of their core beliefs. Many of the people who attend his rallies are authoritarian (working class and otherwise), nativists, anti-Semites, racists, angry, alienated, and animated by feelings of victimhood and resentment of elites who they believe look down upon them.

As a cult leader, Trump gives expression to the feelings of the crowds in his rallies, intensifies them, and further radicalizes them. If you look at the expressions on the faces of the people at Trump's rallies, they often nod in agreement at his statements and accept, with little reservations, his countless lies and falsehoods in the post-truth climate of opinion that Trump espouses.

They seem to have a sense that they have important information that others do not have, which generates in them a kind of messianic intensity that manifests itself in their extreme behavior. Trump has politicized wearing masks and becoming vaccinated and just about every other aspect of life. Hyper-politicization is a hallmark of authoritarian regimes.

In Le Bon's discussion of electoral crowds in *The Crowd*, he reminds us that leaders exercise control over crowds by contagion, repetition, affirmation, and prestige, as well as making fantastic promises that are not binding. Elsewhere in the book, Le Bon mentions that leaders of crowds often are persons with a narrow focus, who use simplistic language, and who are often not highly educated.

The signs prominently shown in Trump's rallies, the people with Trump flags and Trump MAGA hats, the prominent display of the American flag, and all the other signifiers of Trump create a powerful tool for indoctrinating people and intensifying their ideological preferences.

Chapter 6

CROWDS AND AMERICAN
NATIONAL CHARACTER

Scholars and writers often speculate on American exceptionalism, the notion that America differs from other countries and that because of our history, spiritual values, economic wealth, and military power, we have a special obligation to lead the world in many areas.

On September 25, 2015, David Brooks, a columnist for *The New York Times,* had a column titled "The American Idea," which starts off as follows:

> America was settled, founded and built by people who believed they were doing something exceptional. Other nations were defined by their history, but America was defined by its future, by the people who weren't yet here and by the greatness that hadn't yet been achieved.

Later in the column, he argues that the conservative Republican politicians who talk about American exceptionalism are destroying the concept by looking backwards to an imagined America, an America that was not multicultural and mixed race and that was not full of immigrants from Europe, Asia, and Africa and everyplace else.

The image of America in the minds of the Republican politicians Brooks was writing about is of a fantasied America made up primarily of White Anglo-Saxon Protestants (WASPS) living in farms and small towns and not in an America with huge cities full of people from many other countries with many skin colors and religions. It turns out that over sixty percent of Americans live in cities and only seven percent of Americans live on farms.

Anyone who has traveled to countries in Europe, Asia, and South America can tell you people in the various countries in these continents are all different from one another in many ways, such as their skin color, body shapes, the languages they speak, the food they eat, the clothes they wear, the way they have sex, their racial makeup, and the religions they practice.

Figure 6.1 People at a Football Game in a huge stadium.

The term we use for the differences we find in countries as far as personality is concerned is national character. What national character suggests is that where we are born and grow up plays an important role in the way we think and behave.

Nations differ from one another in various ways, and parts or regions of countries differ from other parts of the same country in important ways. I recall reading a description of a book by a geographer who argued that there are seven different Americas, such as, for example, the New England America, the Pacific Northwest America, the Midwest America, the Deep South America, the Atlantic states America (such as New York and New Jersey), and so on. So place matters when it comes to variations on national character (Figure 6.1).

National Character

A French psychoanalyst and marketing consultant, Clotaire Rapaille, wrote a book in 2006 that helps us to understand how countries differ (Figure 6.2). His book is titled *The Culture Code: An Ingenious Way to Understand Why People around the World Live and Buy as They Do*. In this book, he suggests that children from the age of one to seven are "imprinted"

Clotaire Rapaille

Figure 6.2 Clotaire Rapaille.

by the places in which they grow up and this imprinting helps shape their behavior for the rest of their lives.

He writes (2006: 21):

> Most of us imprint the meanings of the things most central to our lives by the age of seven. This is because emotion is the central force for children under the age of seven.

Rapaille believes that three kinds of unconscious shape our behavior: A Freudian individual unconscious, a Jungian collective unconscious, and a cultural unconscious, which represents the codes imprinted on us by growing up in a country that shape our behavior. He explains the relationship that exists between codes as imprints (2006:11):

> An imprint and its Code are like a lock and its combination. If you have all the right numbers in the right sequence, you can open the lock.

Doing so over a vast array of imprints has profound implications. It brings to us the answer to one of our most fundamental questions: why do we act the way we do? Understanding the Culture Code provides us with a remarkable new tool—a new set of glasses, if you will, with which to view ourselves and our behaviors. It changes the way we see everything around us. What's more, it confirms what we have always suspected is true—that, despite our common humanity, people around the world really *are* different. The Culture Code offers a way to understand how.

The Culture Code discusses differences between Americans and people in other cultures. They all have been imprinted by different codes that affect their behavior. This explains why the children of immigrants become Americans so easily. If they are young enough, they become "imprinted" with American cultural codes. For their older brothers and sisters, the process is a bit more difficult, but human beings are very adaptable and if they attend our schools, they can learn the codes and adapt.

Since their parents have been imprinted with the codes of the country where they grew up and lived, it is more difficult for them to adjust to American culture—but it is not impossible and millions of immigrants in America have integrated themselves into the fabric of American society. This is not the case in France where the Muslim immigrants, for a variety of reasons, have not been integrated into French culture.

What is important to realize is that every culture has its codes and finding the codes that inform each culture helps us understand why people in that culture act the way they do. For example, Rapaille says that the American code for food is FUEL because we regard the body as a machine that must be kept going. That explains why at the end of a meal in America we say "I'm full," while in France, where people have a different attitude toward food, people say "that was delicious." He points out that in 2005 Americans spent a hundred billion dollars on fast food, though he recognizes that there are many "foodies" (people who love fine food) in the United States.

There are, then, different codes for different activities in each country and young children are "imprinted" with the codes and these codes generally guide their behavior for the rest of their lives. These codes can be described as "the way we do things here" and there are also codes for France, China, Japan, wherever and what we call culture can be understood to be the numerous codes for everything that are imprinted upon us as we grow up. It is possible, of course, for people to move to other countries and learn different codes, but mostly, the way we live, as Americans or Germans or Japanese is based on the codes we learned as we grew up in America, Germany or Japan.

Figure 6.3 Geoffrey Gorer.

Geoffrey Gorer defines national character in his book *The People of Great Russia: A Psychological Study* (Figure 6.3). He writes, in the Introduction to the book, about the way cultures maintain themselves (1961: xxxix):

If we accept the fact that all the peoples of the world are human, with the same physiology and the same psychological potentialities, whatever their present level of technological development, system of values, or political organization, and that all human beings are organized into societies with distinctive cultures, then all human beings and human societies can be studied, at least potentially, by scientific techniques which have been developed to these ends. Of these scientific techniques, social anthropology and whole-person psychology (including depth psychology and developmental data of ethology) are the most appropriate. Psychology has shown that in the life of any individual the process of learning is cumulative, so that early learning influences later learning; social anthropology has shown that culture is continuous over more than one generation, that the people who die are replaced by new members who have learned, by both conscious and unconscious processes, the values and customs appropriate to their culture and their position in it, or, in other words, their individual variation of the national character.

So, there is such a thing as a national character but there are also countless individual variations on this character caused by any number of factors: where one was born, where someone grows up, one's race, religion, and socioeconomic status, and so on.

In his book, *The American People*, Gorer has a chapter titled "Europe and the Rejected Father" that argues that Americans, many of whom are immigrants or the children of immigrants, see themselves as different from their European (and other) fatherlands and reject the European father figure in their families as the source of moral authority. This parallels the rejection of England by early Americans. We tend to see authority as arbitrary, despotic, and coercive.

As Gorer explains (1964:30):

> From the emergence of America as an independent nation, two major themes appear as characteristic of Americans: the emotional egalitarianism which maintains that all (white American) men are equal to the extent that the subordination of one man to another is repugnant and legally forbidden, equal in opportunity and legal position; and the belief that authority over people is morally detestable and should be resisted.

An American historian, Frederick Jackson Turner, had a hypothesis similar to Gorer's notion of the rejected Europe (Figure 6.4). Turner's thesis is that American culture and character are unique because of the American frontier, which did not end until 1890. According to Turner, the frontier filtered out European influences and institutions (and those from other countries as well) so that a genuinely original and distinctive American culture developed here. Turner's opponents looked to Europe, not to the Frontier (and Nature) as the source of American culture.

Turner described this process in the following manner in "The Frontier in American History." As he explained (1893:1):

> Up to our own day, American history has been in a large degree the history of the colonization of the Great West. The existence of an area of free land, its continuous recession, and the advance of American settlement explain American development. Behind institutions, behind constitutional forms and modifications, lie the **vital forces** (my emphasis) that call these organs into life and shape them to meet challenging conditions. The peculiarity of American institutions is, the fact that they have been compelled to adapt themselves to the changes of an expanding people.

He adds that although there has been a germ of European influence upon America, the advance of the frontier has meant a steady movement away from the influence of Europe, and a steady growth of independence in American

Figure 6.4 Frederick Jackson Turner.

lives. And to study this advance, the men who grew up on the frontier, and social results of the frontier, is to study the really American part of our history.

Ultimately, Turner concludes that democracy, nationalism, individualism, equality, as well as other American traits, developed out of the frontier. As he puts it (1893:37) "The result is that to the frontier the American intellect owes its striking characteristics."

Gorer's discussion calls to mind Alexis de Tocqueville's *Democracy in America*, which suggests that equality is the core value from which other traits of the American character spring (Figure 6.5). He writes (1956:26, but originally published in 1835):

> Amongst the novel objects that attracted my attention during my stay in the United States, nothing struck me more forcibly than the general condition of equality among the people. I readily discovered the prodigious influence which this primary fact exercises on the whole course of society; it gives a particular direction to public opinion, and a peculiar tenor to the laws; it imparts new maxims to the governing authorities, and peculiar habits to the governed.

Later in the book, he coins the term "individualism" and discusses the role of individualism in American society, a trait that is tied to equality.

Figure 6.5 Alexis de Tocqueville.

It is only in egalitarian societies, Tocqueville believes, that individualism can flourish, though there is also the danger of conformity and sheepish imitation in egalitarian societies. He discusses the dangers of individualism when it is pushed to extremes (1956:192–193):

> Individualism is a mature and calm feeling, which disposes each member of the community to sever himself from the mass of his fellows, and to draw apart with his family and friends; so that, after he has thus formed a little circle of his own, he willingly leaves society at large to itself. Selfishness originates in blind instinct; individualism proceeds from erroneous judgment more than from depraved feelings; it originates as much in deficiencies of mind as in perversity of heart.

So, we have two important forces that led to the molding of American national character: egalitarianism and individualism. Gorer, like de Tocqueville, saw egalitarianism as of central importance and, like Turner, he saw Americans as people who have cast off their European roots.

Gorer also was interested in the way Americans raised their children, since it has been said that the child is the father of the man. When he discusses how Americans raise children in a chapter titled, "The All-American Child," he points out that in the United States, mothers dominate the raising of children and that parental love is conditional—based on the child's success with its peers. American children become used to recounting their experiences to their parents and find that what they say generates either love or the withdrawal of love, praise, or blame. This leads children to (1964:88):

Speak overemphatically, to exaggerate, to boast. The parents are so used to this (they did it themselves) that they allow it to go unchecked, mentally making the calculations which will separate the kernel of true achievement from the husk of infantile self-glorification and self-dramatization.

Later in the chapter, he discusses the ideas of Margaret Mead that American children feel hostile to and resent newborn siblings because the older children have to abandon their progress toward independence. He writes that 1964:95):

From this initial situation she derives "the bitterness towards all those who 'have it soft,' 'get by,' 'get away with murder,' a bitterness combined with envy."

In his next chapter, "On Love and Friendship," Gorer offers another important insight relative to crowds and their leaders. He points out that (1964:107):

Love in America [...] tends to have a nonreciprocal quality: to be loved it is not necessary to love in return, but rather to be worthy of love. [...] Because the child is pushed to the very limit of its capacity, because the conditions for success are often so vague, or so far outside its control, the child becomes insatiable for the signs of love, reassuring it that it is worthy of love, and therefore a success.

When I read this material, I could not help but think of the relationship that exists between Trump and his followers and of the commonly made assertions about loyalty with Trump being nonreciprocal.

I might also suggest that Trump's many rallies are attempts he makes, probably without being conscious of what is going on, to convince himself that he is worthy of love and is a success. That is why the size of the crowds he attracts is so important to him. The size of his crowds appeals to his vanity but also his unconscious need for acceptance and admiration.

It is also possible to see the relationship between Trump and his crowds in terms of codependency, which is defined in Wikipedia as follows:

> In sociology, **codependency** is a concept that attempts to characterize imbalanced relationships where one person enables another person's self-destructive tendencies (such as addiction, poor mental health, immaturity, irresponsibility, or under-achievement) and/or undermines the other person's relationship.[1] Definitions of codependency vary but typically include high self-sacrifice, a focus on others' needs, suppression of one's own emotions, and attempts to control or fix other people's problems.[2] People who self-identify as codependents exhibit low self-esteem, but it is unclear whether this is a cause or an effect of characteristics associated with codependency.[3] Codependency is generally defined as a subclinical, situational, and/or episodic behavioral condition similar to that of dependent personality disorder. Codependency is not limited to married, partnered or romantic relationships as co-workers, friends and family can be codependent.
>
> (https://en.wikipedia.org/wiki/Codependency)

If Trump and the crowds at his rallies are seen as codependent, we have a situation in which Trump enables his followers at his rallies to indulge in self-destructive thoughts and in some cases behavior, and his followers encourage Trump to continue behaving the way he does. This is a hypothesis worth considering.

Are American Crowds Distinctive

If there is such a thing as national character and Americans are different in important ways from people in other countries, we must ask ourselves—are American crowds different from crowds in other countries, or are all crowds more or less the same? Is there something about being a member of a crowd that nullifies national character, which means that French crowds, English crowds, Japanese crowds, and crowds everywhere are similar to one another and all are similar to American crowds? (Figure 6.6).

If you believe all crowds are essentially alike, you have to assume that some kind of group psychology takes over and, just as Le Bon argues, people lose their sense of individuality and become captivated by a kind of universal group mind.

It would seem to me that if there is such a thing as national character, this character would manifest itself in the behavior of national crowds, and a crowd full of egalitarian and individualistic Americans would differ

Figure 6.6 A crowd in a Football Stadium.

from a crowd in countries with a feudal background and an aristocracy, such as France or Japan. Maybe the growth of the mass media and social media has flattened the differences between countries so that we are all become more or less the same, but that hypothesis does not strike me as supportable.

In Table 6.1, I contrast American beliefs about themselves and about Europe that suggest that Americans see themselves as different from people in their fatherlands.

The American poet Ralph Waldo Emerson wrote a poem, "America, My Country," in which he described it as a land without history:

Land without history, land lying all
In the plain daylight of the temperate zone,
The plain acts
Without exaggeration done in day:
Thy interests contested by their manifold good sense.
In their own clothes without the ornament
Of bannered Army harnessed in uniform.
Land where, and 'tis in Europe counted a reproach
Land without nobility, or wigs, or debt.
No castles, no cathedrals, and no kings.
Land of the forest.

Table 6.1 America/Europe bipolar oppositions.

America	Europe
Nature	History
Individualism	Conformity
Innocence	Guilt
The future	The past
Hope	Memory
Forests	Cathedrals
Cowboy	Cavalier
Willpower	Class conflict
Equality	Hierarchy (Aristocracy, Feudalism)
Achievement	Ascription
Classless society	Class-bound society
Nature food, raw food	Gourmet food
Clean living	Sensuality
Action	Theory
Agrarianism	Industrialism
The Sacred	The Profane

This poem reflects the way Americans see themselves—or saw themselves for many years: no remnants of feudalism, no official religions, no hereditary aristocracy, and living in nature. This poem reflects an idealized view of American society and culture and one that, in certain respects, we still believe in, even though it may no longer be accurate. Most Americans live in cities now, not in "the forest," and the country is most certainly are not without debt, but in our imaginations, we are still an agrarian nation full of people in small towns living in nature.

Table 6.1 would suggest that there are two kinds of crowds: American crowds with an American mentality and value system and the kinds of crowds found in Europe and other countries with different mentalities and values.

Chapter 7

CROWDS AND THE JANUARY 6, 2021 INSURRECTION

Along with 9/11 when the World Trade Center buildings were destroyed by terrorists using airplanes as missiles, 1/6 is a day of monumental importance in American history. But unlike 9/11, the terrorists attacking the Capitol building were not foreign terrorists but American ones.

The attack on the Capitol raises a question: when does a crowd become a mob? The answer would seem to be that when a crowd becomes highly motivated and excited and loses its sense of moral composure, it becomes a mob (Figure 3.2).

Le Bon has a chapter on "Crowds Termed Criminal Crowds?" in which he explains that the people who take part in these crowds/mobs are open to suggestion and believe they are acting "in obedience to a duty," which with the 1/6 insurrection was following Trump's and several other Republican politicians' instructions to "fight like hell" and, by implication, prevent Joe Biden, who it was said had stolen the election, from being installed as president.

Many of the members of the mob that attacked the Capitol on 1/6 have said that they believed they were acting on the orders of President Trump and that their behavior was not criminal but the behavior of true patriots.

An article, "90 Seconds of Rage on the Capitol Steps" by Dan Barry, Alan Feuer, and Matthew Rosenberg, on the first page of the Sunday edition of *The New York Times,* describe the behavior of seven rioters who worked in concert perpetrating violence for 90 seconds during the riot (October 17, 2021: 1):

[...] Prosecutors and congressional investigators seem to understand how a political rally devolved into an assault on the citadel of American democracy and those who guard it. They are drilling down on whether the riot was organized and what roles were played by far-right extremist groups, various Trump supporters and Mr. Trump himself.

But it may also help to slow down the video evidence, linger on those 90 seconds on the Capitol steps and trace back the roots of the violence and its perpetrators. Doing so provides a close-up view of how seemingly average citizens—duped by a political lie, goaded by their leaders, and swept up in a frenzied mob—can unite in breathtaking acts of brutality.

Most of the rioters were described by the authors as (October 17, 2021: 22):

> Whiter, slightly older and less likely than the general population to live in a city or be college-educated. Recent studies indicate that they come from places where people tend to fear the replacement of their ethnic community and cultural dominance by immigrants, and adhere to the false belief that the 2020 election was stolen.

It is reasonable to suggest that the people at the rally—not highly educated, small town or rural, believers in conspiracy theories, afraid that they were being "replaced" by immigrants, and feeling a loss of status—were more susceptible than the average person or than college-educated people to manipulation by Trump and his colleagues. We are left with the question about the suggestibility of crowds and whether the socioeconomic and educational status of people in a crowd has an impact upon the way a crowd behaves. If it is correct that a crowd doesn't have to be in one place, it means that thanks to the Internet and the mass media, many people can be members of a crowd, forming what we can describe as a virtual crowd. And this widespread crowd can be affected by mind control tactics and turned into a political cult—and with its embrace of QAnon, also a religious cult. I discussed this topic earlier but I think that the Trump followers who attacked the Capitol building were motivated by both politics and a religious sense involving what they believed that nothing less than the salvation of the American way of life, as the insurrectionists saw things, was at stake. This explains the mob's fury. An article in *The New York Times* by Elizabeth Dias, "Extremism From Whites Has Strong Roots in U.S." deals with this matter (Monday, February 8, 2021: A11):

> Many rioters, a largely white group, were motivated by religious fervor and saw themselves as participants in a kind of holy war. Some brought Confederate flags, others crosses. […] In many ways it resembled the culture of the Ku Klux Klan in the 1920's.

Americans had ample opportunity to watch the assault on the Capitol, which was displayed widely on television. They could watch the way the mob attacked the guards, broke into the offices of prominent Democrats, and screamed that they wanted to find Nancy Pelosi and kill her and do the same for Vice President Mike Pence. Scenes from the riot are repeated regularly on news programs.

An October 15, 2021, article in *The Wall Street Journal* by Dorothy Rabinowitz describes the insurrection as follows. The title of the article in *Day of Rage, Insurrection and Infamy* is a review of a TV program, "Four Hours at the Capitol" that was broadcast by HBO and HBO Max (2021: A11):

> There's little that can be called surprising about the passions that drove Trump supporters to storm the U.S. Capitol this January in protest of Joe Biden's certification as the winner of the 2020 presidential election—an invasion that caused lawmakers to crouch under their desks and reach for gas masks. […] The most unforgettable sequences by far are the ones of violence visited on the police by the insurrectionist crowds battling to get into the Capitol—brutality both prolonged and aglow with fevered exhibitionism.

And now, in recent weeks, in a scene out of Orwell's *1984*, members of the Republican Party have told the American public not to believe what they saw and argued that what the American public saw was not a riot and that the insurrectionists who attacked the Capitol and injured many of the Capitol police should be seen as patriots and not criminals. Many Republicans deny that there was a riot. One of Orwell's characters in his novel *1984* had a job rewriting history and the members of the Republican Party, who are downgrading the riot (one Republican member of the house described the rioters as orderly tourists), are acting like characters in *1984*. A select committee in the House of Representatives, with two Republicans and the rest Democrats, is trying to get information that will explain who financed the riot, what role Trump and any other Republican politicians played in the event, what Trump was doing while the riot was going on, and other pertinent information. The committee is trying to obtain phone records, written material, and other information that will enable them to determine what role Trump and certain other Republicans played in the events leading up to the riot and perhaps in the riot itself.

This investigation is occurring as the country faces an election in November 2022 and time is of the essence, since, if the Republicans take control of the house, they will shut down the investigation. The Democrats hope that what they find may play a role in the election and swing it in their direction.

Whatever the case, there is high drama in America as the Democrats face what they believe is an existential threat to democracy in America in 2022 and 2024 if Trump runs and wins the presidency.

Chapter 8

CROWDS AND COVID

The question this chapter discusses involves why so many people in America refuse to get vaccinated. We find the same reluctance to be vaccinated in other countries but not to the extent that vaccine resistance exists in the United States. In the United States now, since we developed vaccines, almost all of the people dying from Covid-19 are unvaccinated (over 90%) so we must wonder whether they form some kind of death cult, made up of followers of Donald J. Trump.When the virus first appeared, Trump paid little attention to it, saying that it was like the flu. He wasted precious months getting the vaccine out to people and told his followers not to wear masks and not to get vaccinated—though he was vaccinated and that probably saved his life since he caught the disease and ended up at Walter Reed Hospital where he received special treatments. He came very close to dying.

If Angela Merkel Were in Charge in America

Germany has a population of about 83 million people and it is estimated that as of October 2021, around 94,000 Germans have died from the virus. The United States has a population of 329 million people and as of October 2021 around 770,000 Americans have died from the virus. America has approximately three times as many people as Germany.

    If Germany had the same population as the United States and we multiply 83 million times three to get approximately 329 million people, around 282 thousand people would have died, so if Angela Merkel and her German colleagues had been running the United States vaccination program, instead of Trump, around 500,000 Americans would still be alive.

	USA Trump in Charge	**USA Merkel in Charge**
Population	329 million	329 million
Covid deaths	770,000	282,000

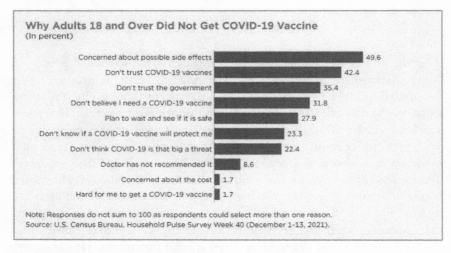

Figure 8.1 Rationales of Covid-19 skeptics. U.S. Census Bureau.

Some of the 777,000 deaths occurred after the vaccines were developed and distributed, which means the epidemic of Covid deaths since then are mostly from the unvaccinated (Figure 8.1).

Rationales of the Unvaccinated

One reason many people have not been vaccinated in America is that wearing masks and becoming vaccinated have become part of the hyper-politicization that is part of the Trump program. Under Trump, everything possible has been politicized, so not wearing masks and not getting vaccinated became political statements rather than public health imperatives.

The misinformation carried on Fox News and some Facebook and other social media postings have further exacerbated the problem. Trump championed medicines that were not effective and, sometimes, dangerous. For example, many Trump supporters purchased a remedy of parasites in horses at farm supply stores. Several people who took it died, but that did not hamper the passion for the medicine from Trump supporters. He also wondered whether injecting bleach would be a useful procedure, which suggests a profound lack of understanding of biology and was a major embarrassment. Many evangelical Christians rejected taking the vaccine on religious grounds, but there is a reason to suspect that the real reason for their behavior is that they are fervent Trump supporters. Interviews with Trump supporters reveal that many of them make spurious arguments about the vaccine being rushed, about it not being effective, about it not being tested long enough, and similar arguments. These arguments are, I would suggest, rationalizations that people make to support their not being vaccinated. Of course, there are also anti-Vax groups that are against all vaccinations. Many Trump supporters live in information silos and only watch Fox TV (in essence, the propaganda arm of the Republican Party) or other right-wing stations and thus have been fed misinformation and lies about the disease and the vaccinations. The news stations are full of interviews with people dying of Covid-19 who say they were lied to by Fox or other networks and make deathbed conversions, except that it is too late. One argument people make is that mandates are impinging upon their personal liberty. What they do not acknowledge is that their "freedom" not to take the vaccines or not to have to take the vaccines impinges upon the freedom of the majority of Americans who have been vaccinated. The hospitals throughout the country are full of people who have not been vaccinated and are dying of Covid-19. There are so many of them that people who need operations cannot get them because so many of the beds in Intensive Care units are full of people sick from the virus.

An article by Zeynep Tufekci, "The Unvaccinated May Not Be Who You Think They Are," which appeared in the October 16, 2021 issue of *The New York Times* offers some information into the makeup of the unvaccinated. It has information from The Covid States Project which finds two groups, almost equal in number, of people in the United States: the "vaccine willing" and the vaccine-resistant. As Tufkekci explains (2021: A 19):

> Its research finds that the unvaccinated don't have much trust in institutions and authorities: only 39 percent of the unvaccinated trust hospitals and doctors "a lot," for example, while 71 percent of the vaccinated do.
>
> This mistrust may be fueled not only by relentless propaganda against public health measures but by the sorry state of health care in this country.

In the report, we find that some people did not get vaccinated because of medical problems they had, such as heart murmurs or diabetes, some worried about the side effects of the vaccines, some have a fear of needles, and Black people and minorities are worried about the way the government has mistreated them in the past. Tufekci lays part of the responsibility on the government not dealing with personal anxieties adequately and concludes the article writing (2021:A19):

> We need to develop a realistic, informed and deeply pragmatic approach to our shortcomings without ceding ground to the conspirators, grifters and demagogues.

On the Madness of Crowds

In 1841, Charles Mackay published a book on *Extraordinary Popular Delusions and the Madness of Crowds*. This review comes from Wikipedia.

> ***Extraordinary Popular Delusions and the Madness of Crowds*** is an early study of crowd psychology by Scottish journalist Charles Mackay, first published in 1841 under the title *Memoirs of Extraordinary Popular Delusions*.[1] The book was published in three volumes: "National Delusions," "Peculiar Follies," and "Philosophical Delusions."[2] Mackay was an accomplished teller of stories, though he wrote in a journalistic and somewhat sensational style.
>
> The subjects of Mackay's debunking include alchemy, crusades, duels, economic bubbles, fortune-telling, haunted houses, the Drummer of Tedworth, the influence of politics and religion on the shapes of beards and hair, magnetisers (influence of imagination in curing disease), murder through poisoning, prophecies, popular admiration of great thieves, popular follies of great cities, and relics. Present-day writers on economics, such as Michael Lewis and Andrew Tobias, laud the three chapters on economic bubbles.[3]

n.wikipedia.org/wiki/Extraordinary_Popular_Delusions_and_the_
Madness_of_Crowds

What we learn from Mackay is the crowds have always been open to crazy ideas, delusions, and a kind of madness that sometimes manifests itself in considering diseases and quack medical remedies. So people believe in useless medicines and taking medicines that are ineffective or dangerous, or both is nothing new. Snake oil peddlers go way back into our history and the history of other countries. The fact that some people in other countries also feel hostile to mandates, as well as conventional medical remedies for Covid-19, suggests that the American perspective on these matters is not confined to our borders. Other groups in many foreign countries feel the same way about mandates, though they may also be animated by right-wing political beliefs. For example, many Russians are vaccine-hesitant or refuse to be vaccinated. An article in the October 19, 2021 edition of *The New York Times* titled "Russia Has Its Own Vaccine. Most Russians Have No Interest in Taking It," by Valerie Hopkins points out that many Russians do not believe the Russian Sputnik V is effective and do not trust the government. Hopkins quotes some Russians, who suggest that a combination of a diminished sense of social responsibility and the development of individualism and a diminished sense of the public good have contributed to Russia's failure to vaccinate a high percentage of the population. Mandates seem to be working, generally speaking. What will happen with the small group of people who refuse to be vaccinated remains to be seen. We might attain herd immunity without them, though their existence continues to pose a challenge to the American political order and the health and well-being of American society.

Why people behave the way they do continues to be enigmatic and our best minds—philosophers, psychologists, sociologists, anthropologists, novelists, and one could add to this list endlessly—have, for thousands of years, tried to understand what motivates people and how we can change people's beliefs and behavior in positive ways.

One of the more enigmatic aspects of resistance to vaccination involves medical professionals. A story in the Saturday/Sunday edition of *The Wall Street Journal* (Page 1) is titled "Vaccine or Get Fired? These Nurses Say No," explains that many nurses "distrust the system, fear long-term health effects and bristle at mandates and believe mandates that require vaccinations," (Page A11) which they believe "impinge on their liberties." Doctors are a different story, where ninety seven percent of all doctors in the United States have been vaccinated.

In the case of the Covid virus, we must find ways to shape people's behavior because their survival and our survival, in the face of a deadly pandemic, are dependent upon our being able to do so. It is important since many people who refuse to become vaccinated are dying from Covid-19, so we are having trouble convincing people to do something to save their lives.Freudian psychoanalytic theory has elaborated a theory about death wishes. Wikipedia describes it as follows:

> In classical Freudian psychoanalytic theory, the **death drive** (German: *Todestrieb*) is the drive toward death and destruction, often expressed through behaviors such as aggression, repetition compulsion, and self-destructiveness.[1][2] It was originally proposed by Sabina Spielrein in her paper "Destruction as the Cause of Coming Into Being"[3][4] (*Die Destruktion als Ursache des Werdens*)[5] in 1912, which was then taken up by Sigmund Freud in 1920 in *Beyond the Pleasure Principle*. This concept has been translated as "opposition between the ego or death instincts and the sexual or life instincts."[6] In *Pleasure Principle*, Freud used the plural "death drives" (*Todestriebe*) much more frequently than the singular.[7] The death drive opposes Eros, the tendency toward survival, propagation, sex, and other creative, life-producing drives. The death drive is sometimes referred to as "Thanatos" in post-Freudian thought, complementing "Eros," although this term was not used in Freud's own work, being rather introduced by Wilhelm Stekel in 1909 and then by Paul Federn in the present context.[8][9] Subsequent psychoanalysts such as Jacques Lacan and Melanie Klein have defended the concept.
>
> (https://en.wikipedia.org/wiki/Death_drive)

It is possible to think about the self-destructive behavior of the people refusing to be vaccinated as a collective manifestation of the death drive. The news shows offer many reports of non-vaccinated people dying from Covid-19 who claim that they have the flu and not Covid-19. Even on their death beds, they cannot admit to the truth about their illnesses. This is an extreme example of the denial—the notion that "it can't happen to me" that affects the thinking of many who refuse to be vaccinated.

We can see that there are many explanations possible to describe the behavior of the Trump following crowd and its Covid-19 relationship. Whatever the explanation, the Trumpian crowds pose a danger to themselves and society. The people who refuse to be vaccinated have no sense of responsibility to others, no sense of a public good, and pose a problem that, to this point, nobody has solved.

There is one fact which, whether for good or ill, is of utmost importance in the public life of Europe at the present moment. This fact is the accession of the masses to complete social power. As the masses, by definition, neither should nor can direct their own personal existence, and still less rule society in general, the fact means that actually Europe is suffering from the greatest crisis that can afflict peoples, nations, and civilization. It is called the rebellion of the masses. In order to understand this formidable fact, it is important to avoid giving to the words "rebellion," "masses," and "social power" a meaning exclusively or primarily political. Public life is not solely political, but equally, and even primarily, intellectual, moral, economic religious; it comprises all our collective habits, including our fashions both of dress and amusement. The individuals who made up these multitudes existed, but not *qua* multitude. Scattered about the world in small groups, or solitary, they lived a life, to all appearances, divergent, dissociate, apart. Each individual or small group occupied a place, its own, in country, village, town, or quarter of the great city. Now, suddenly, they appear as an agglomeration, and looking in any direction our eyes meet with multitudes. The multitude has suddenly become visible, installing itself in the preferential positions in society.

Jose Ortega y Gasset, *The Revolt of the Masses*. 1930.

Chapter 9

CODA

I can only wonder what Ortega y Gasset would have thought had he been able to observe the divisive and corrosive nature of contemporary American politics and read my book on crowds. He wrote his book in 1932, but his ideas seem oddly relevant today—in part because he recognized the problems generated by the emergence of the "multitudes" or what Le Bon would call the crowd. It was Trump's behavior—and the behavior of his angry followers who attacked the Capitol that led me to write this book. Bob Woodward and Robert Costa conclude their book, *Peril*, as follows (2021:418):

> Five years ago, on March 31, 2016, when Trump was on the verge of winning the Republican presidential, we worked together for the first time and interviewed Trump as his then unfinished Trump International Hotel on Pennsylvania Avenue in Washington. That day we recognized he was an extraordinary political force, in many ways right out of the American playbook. An outsider. Anti-Establishment. A builder. Bombastic. Confident. A fast-talking scrapper. But we also saw darkness. He could be petty. Cruel. Bored by American history and dismissive of governing traditions that had long guided elected leaders. Tantalized by the prospect of power. Eager to use fear to get his way. "Real power is—I don't even want to use the word—rear," Trump told us. "I bring rage out. I do bring rage out. I always have. I don't know if that's an asset or a liability, but whatever it is, I do." Could Trump work his will again? Were there any limits to what he has his supporters might do to put him back in power? Peril remains.

That is the situation we face now in America as our democratic institutions are in peril from Trump and the Republican Party, which has become an antidemocratic cult of Trump followers—or is the term "worshipers" more accurate?

INDEX

CPSIA information can be obtained
at www.ICGtesting.com
Printed in the USA
JSHW021639170423
40437JS00001B/7